Lillehammer'94

CANADA'S OLYMPIC STORIES

ROD BLACK

PHOTOGRAPHS BY
D.H.(DON) METZ

CANADA

THE OFFICIAL
COMMEMORATIVE
BOOK OF THE XVII
WINTER GAMES

ISBN: 1-8960-9202-0

INFACT Publishing Ltd.
66 Portland St.
2nd Floor
Toronto, ON
M5V 2M8

INFACT Publishing Ltd. is an official licensee of the Canadian Olympic Association.
Represented by the Canadian Manda Group

JACKET AND TEXT DESIGN AND VIDEO DIGITIZATION: Brant Cowie/ArtPlus Limited

Cover photograph of Susan Auch appears with the permission of The Landmark Group; Cover photograph of Myriam Bédard appears with the permission of Jean-Marc St-Pierre Sport Marketing Inc.; Cover photograph of Jean-Luc Brassard appears with the permission of The Landmark Group; Cover photograph of Isabelle Brasseur and Lloyd Eisler appears with the permission of IMG; Cover photograph of Kurt Browning appears with the permission of IMG Canada; Cover photograph of Edi Podivinsky appears with the permission of IMG Canada; Cover photograph of Elvis Stojko appears with the permission of Futerman & Futerman.

Printed in Canada by Metropole Litho

CONTENTS

The XVIIth Olympic Winter Games in Lillehammer represented a special time for all Canadians.

During sixteen splendid days in Norway, our athletes realized their lifelong goal of Olympic competition. Here at home, Canadians were treated to a spectacle of stunning athleticism. From the Olympic Park to the Hakan Hall, we celebrated with great pride the achievements of our country's best athletes and their commitment to excellence. Many of the moments that stirred our emotions have been captured here, in Lillehammer '94: Canada's Olympic Stories.

The Games were an event worthy of celebration. The years of personal sacrifice and arduous training were rewarded as the Canadian team distinguished itself with the nation's best-ever results at an Olympic Winter Games. But more than that, our athletes demonstrated a sense of sportsmanship and camaraderie that is the essence of the Olympic spirit.

The legacy of the Games will be our collective pride, and our shared memories are a guarantee that the Olympic dream will continue.

Jean Chrétien
Prime Minister of Canada

1994 was the second time that the Winter Olympic Games took place in Norway. The first time was in Oslo in 1952. The Lillehammer Games, however, had a much greater impact. This time we took it upon us to show the world some of our ideals with regards to sports and, hopefully, we succeeded.

I believe the Olympic Games at Lillehammer turned out to be what we Norwegians wanted them to be: A sports festival with athletes in focus, but also with reflections on the tragedy in Sarajevo and on other conflicts around the world.

The whole point of the Olympic movement is to provide a venue where the world's best athletes meet, compete, represent their countries with honour and get to know each other in an atmosphere of peace.

In Norway, we have an old saying which goes, "What is important is not to win, but to take part in the competition." It is through honest competition that we learn to respect not only the winners but also those who do not win. You probably remember from TV how the spectators cheered for everybody, Norwegian or foreigner, winners as well as losers.

The sports feast would, however, not have attracted so much attention without the winners and their dedication. Canada had many winners. I was truly impressed by the width and depth of Canadian winter sports. Traditionally, we have thought of hockey and skating as Canada's winter activities and, in those sports, you lived up to what the world expected. It was perhaps the single most dramatic event of the Games when the Canadian hockey team lost the final with the narrowest possible margin. The performance of the Canadian participants in other disciplines was also most impressive.

As Norway's representative in Canada, it was a special pleasure for me to observe how the Games strengthened the bonds between Norway and Canada. The events of these Games reminded us of how much our two countries have in common. Moreover, for the many Canadians with Norwegian roots the Games were an opportunity to renew old ties. For Canadians in general, I hope it was an opportunity to be proud and to become acquainted with Norway and the Norwegian way.

Bjørn Kristvik
Ambassador to Canada
Royal Norwegian Embassy

104 young men and women were chosen to represent Canada at the XVIIth Olympic Games held at Lillehammer in February, 1994. They came from all regions of our country, they represented diverse ethnic and cultural backgrounds and they competed in different events and disciplines. As a team, they were the most successful group of athletes ever to have represented our country in Olympic Winter Games competition. Stories of their performances are chronicled in the photographs and written words that are contained in this book.

The athletes who formed the Canadian Olympic team in Lillehammer are a microcosm of the fabric of our nation. It was interesting for me to be able to witness how important it was for each of the athletes to be a Canadian and to support one another in their common goal, which was to represent themselves, their sport and their country in a manner that would make all of us proud.

It was my privilege as Chef de Mission to lead a team of professionals who provided support services to these athletes. My colleagues would all join me in applauding the manner in which all of the athletes conducted themselves, both on and off the field of play. The stories that follow tell you something about this incredible group of young Canadians.

William J. Warren
Chef de Mission

INTRODUCTION

A few months before the 1994 Winter Olympics, the only thing most of us knew about Lillehammer was that it was about to become the northernmost city to ever host the Games. We had no idea what this rather obscure Norwegian village had in store for us.

There is great mystery preceding any Olympics. Just as a host city can never be sure what kind of legacy it will leave when the flame flickers out, so, too, the fortunes of the athletes can rise or fall. It's unpredictable; you just never know what is going to happen.

That is part of the magic of the Olympics. For sixteen days we watch with suspense and admiration as the best of our athletes take the spotlight. Our conversations become punctuated with replays of games, races and performances. We make an emotional investment in these total strangers on whom so many hopes and dreams are pinned.

Former CTV sports director Johnny Esaw described the Olympic phenomenon to me perfectly a couple of years ago when he said, " The Olympics are unlike anything in sports. They can take you to the moon and back in ten seconds."

He was right. There is no recurring event that captures our imagination so overwhelmingly, or that moves us through such a range of emotions in such a short time as the Olympic Games.

Now, looking back at the Lillehammer Games, we know that Lillehammer left us with something very special. This book springs to life from that feeling. It is a compilation of the memories brought back from Norway, particularly those of our great Canadian athletes who won more medals than any Winter Olympic team in our country's history. These are stories that were told in front of the cameras and those shielded from the glare of the lights. Stories of hope realized and hope dashed. Tears of joy, tears of despair. Olympic stories.

This book is dedicated to the most important part of the Olympics: the athletes. They are the ones who bring out the Olympian in all of us— taking us to the moon and back—with their wins, their losses, their unwavering dedication.

I hope you enjoy this look back at the 17th Winter Olympic Games, as much as I treasured rekindling the memorable moments of those sixteen wonderful days in Lillehammer.

DAY ONE

LET THE GAMES BEGIN

Saturday, February 12, 1994

No one was talking at our table. That was different. For days, whenever we were together, which was practically always, all of us radiated jokes, laughter, gossip, noisy good spirits. But now, 7:30 in the morning over breakfast at the Oyer Gjestegard in Lillehammer, Norway, everyone in the CTV crew was caught in an emotion compounded in about equal parts of charged expectations, butterflies and reined-in excitement. What we were experiencing wasn't exactly the calm before the storm. This was more like the silent anticipation before an opening night on Broadway. The 17th Olympic Winter Games were just eight hours away from its Opening Ceremony, and all of us, the people who were going to broadcast the whole sixteen days and nights of the Games back to Canada, were feeling the enormity of it all.

It was a rush, a thrill, but at this moment, still dark in the February Norwegian morning, silence took over the table.

Six years before not many people had heard of Lillehammer. But somebody from the town must have made a tremendous impression on the International Olympic Committee because in 1988, the Committee announced that Lillehammer would host the Winter Games in 1994.

Once we arrived in town, days before the Olympics began, and got a chance to look the place over, we could appreciate what a wise choice the Committee had made. Lillehammer has the sort of beauty and charm you see on winter postcards. It lies just north of Norway's capital city, Oslo (which hosted the Games in the winter of 1952), and it's in a gorgeous valley called Gudbrandsdalen.

1

This page and next Skydivers before the Games.

The Green Games
Lillehammer organizers used the Olympics to focus world attention on the environment. Venues were built with great care with as few trees as possible cut down in building the sites. Wood, a renewable resource, was a primary construction material. All Olympic print materials used chlorine-free paper. Massive recycling was a part of all aspects of the Games; even the outdoor medal podiums, carved from ice, were recyclable.

Apart from its stunning visual appeal, Lillehammer possesses the one ingredient necessary for winter sports—abundant snow. A year earlier, in 1993, Norway's Olympic people had fretted over the possibility: what if it *doesn't* snow in Gudbrandsdalen in '94? That didn't seem likely, but everybody remembered the near catastrophe at the Games in Innsbruck in the winter of 1964. Snow didn't fly in Austria that year, and the military was pressed into service to truck in tons of the stuff from the northern mountain ranges. Just to avert a replay of that crisis, Lillehammer had Norwegian soldiers and Norwegian trucks on standby. They weren't needed. In fact, by the time the CTV gang reached Lillehammer the roads leading in and out of the village were lined with snow banks that towered ten feet high.

That was one subject all of the newcomers to Norway talked about, the snow, the frigid beauty, the special look of the winter Norwegian countryside. But there was much else for us to discuss and look forward to.

For one thing, these Games promised to be significantly different from past winter competitions. The decision by the International Olympic Committee to stagger the Summer and Winter Games in two-year cycles meant that the Winter Games, held just two years earlier in 1992, came along again in '94. This changed the very nature of these Games. It opened up wonderful opportunities for competitors in the 1992 Games who figured they'd be over the hill by 1996. Not so in '94. They'd still be fresh, still in competitive shape, still primed for a shot at a medal.

Another decision, one made by the International Skating Union, allowed

professionals into the Games. These were people who had enjoyed their golden moments in the Games—or their silver or bronze moments—and then turned pro. The greats of figure skating, the ones who'd set the modern standards for artistry and athleticism were set to return to amateur competition. Brian Boitano. Katarina Witt. Viktor Petrenko. Torvill and Dean. They were coming to Lillehammer, back to the Olympics.

But it wasn't all those mighty performers whose names were on our lips in the days leading up to the Olympics. No way. Everyone was gossiping about the two figure skaters who had, in the previous few weeks, taken over *People* magazine, tabloid TV and a courtroom in Oregon. Nancy Kerrigan and Tonya Harding, of course.

At that point, immediately before the Games, only part of the story had been revealed. We knew that, after a practice session in Cobo Hall in Detroit where the U.S. Nationals were being held, some thug whacked Nancy Kerrigan across the knee. We knew that, with Kerrigan on the disabled list, Tonya Harding went on to win the women's championship. We knew that, as the story unfolded, it was Harding's husband and three men he enlisted who were responsible for attacking Kerrigan in a half-baked scheme that was supposed to pave the way to eventual Olympic gold for Harding. We knew that Harding claimed to have only become aware of the plot after the deed had been done. And we knew that both a recovered Kerrigan and a slightly suspect Harding were on their way to Lillehammer. What we didn't know, nor did anyone else except the principals on Tonya's side, was how closely Harding was really tied to the

Facing page
Kurt Browning
leads the Canadian
contingent.

This page
Scenes from the
Opening Ceremony.

conspiracy. And so the media was waiting in Lillehammer eager to pop their Watergate-type questions at Harding. What did she know? When did she know it?

This was shaping up to be a Winter Olympics like none other.

All of these things, and a few dozen others, were on our minds as we sat, mostly in anticipatory silence at that breakfast on the day the Lillehammer Olympics would begin.

Outside, beyond the dining room, even at that early hour, even in the bone-chilling temperatures, people crowded the streets. Norwegians, I was beginning to appreciate, are a hardy, buoyant people. They revel in the winter atmosphere. They passed the windows in smiling groups, in families, on skis and on contraptions they call "sparks." A spark, for the uninitiated, is similar to a push scooter except that it operates on runners. It's

the favourite mode of winter transportation for Norwegian seniors, and on the streets on this morning of the first day of the 1994 Olympics, men and women in their seventies and eighties buzzed past with the glee of kids on skateboards. Maybe it was this spectacle that got us moving from the breakfast table. We had an Opening Ceremony to cover.

The Ceremony was scheduled for four o'clock in the Olympic Stadium which sits at the base of the Lysgaardsbakkene ski jump. The stadium holds 35,000 people, though many more than that spilled out across the face of the hill beyond the stadium. As the people approached the stadium, filing up the roads in their colourful winter clothes, they created an impression, viewed from a distance, of converging rivers of red and blue and white. But once inside the stadium, they

Lysgårdsbakkene
The Lysgårdsbakkene Ski Jumping Arena at Olympic Park was the venue for the opening and closing ceremonies and the ski jumping and Nordic combined ski jumping events. It could seat 35,000. The site was masterfully integrated into the landscape and served as the focal point for the Olympic gathering.

underwent a fabulous change. That's because, on entering, each person was handed a recyclable white hooded poncho, and when everyone put theirs on and pulled up the hood, the stadium was transformed into a blanket of total white.

Coming up to 4:00 p.m., the snow that had been gently falling began to subside, the air seemed to grow slightly warmer—maybe it was all those happy people converged in one space—and the early twilight fell softly around the stadium. Spotlights swept across the crowd and roamed beyond the stadium to the huge ski jump which loomed over the valley like some manmade monster. The lights cast shadows for hundreds of metres, all the way to Lillehammer. The village itself looked almost eerie, the buildings empty, the streets deserted. Everybody, citizens and visitors, Norwegians and fans from abroad, had

pressed their way to the areas inside and around the stadium.

Finally, at exactly four o'clock, the microphone in the stadium gave off a sharp crack, and the spotlights zeroed in on two men. They were His Excellency Juan Antonio Samaranch and Gerhard Heiberg, respectively, the president of the International Olympic Committee and the president of the Lillehammer Olympic Organizing Committee. But it was neither of these important figures who were to lay first claim to centre stage. According to strict Olympic protocol, the initial order of business in the Opening Ceremony is the entrance of the head of state of the host country. In Norway, that meant the king himself, His Royal Highness Harald V.

Among royalty, Harald is a remarkably open and democratic monarch. CTV's Lloyd

This page and previous The Canadian team enters the Olympic Stadium

Robertson found him to be pleasant, intelligent and unintimidating when he interviewed Harald for the *Norwegian Way* series, and among Norwegians, the king enjoys a reputation as a man who moves around the country, interested, involved, keen to keep in touch with his subjects.

All of which helps to explain the stylish and rather casual entrance that King Harald made into the stadium. Not for him anything that smacked of pomp and pretension. Instead, Harald arrived in a sleigh drawn by four reindeer. The crowd ate it up. So did our cameras. And the king, waving genially, took his place in the royal box.

On centre stage, a snowy centre stage, a children's choir created a powerful image. There were four hundred kids, each wearing five different colours of clothing. When they assumed their final positions, they formed the five Olympic rings, blue, black, red, yellow and green. It was stunning.

Now it was time for the athletes to grace the arena, and on they came. Greece led off the parade, befitting its status as the ancestral homeland of the Ancient Games. The Greeks were followed by sixty-seven participating nations with Norway, the host country, having the honour of concluding the procession.

Kurt Browning led the Canadian contingent, an enormous smile on his face, right hand waving to the crowd, left hand holding the flag aloft. I know that the flag is heavy, but Kurt made his job look effortless. No doubt it was pride and adrenalin that helped him through his key role in the great parade. Kurt, and all the rest of the Canadians, looked absolutely magnificent in their RCMP-inspired outfits: red capes over

Facing page
A scene from the mag-
ical artistic program,
part of the Opening
Ceremony.

This page
Kate Pace and friends
greet Canadians at
home.

red jackets, the word "Canada" etched in gold across their backs, the maple leaf displayed front and centre on their caps. The costumes announced in bold strokes that these great young people were Canadians—and proud of it.

Canadian skier Kate Pace occupied a special role in the parade. At least, she did to CTV. This was our producer John Shannon's brain wave. The Olympic people strictly ban anything from the outside of the athlete's clothing that doesn't relate to the uniform: no advertising, no extra decor, no cameras on straps. The rule makes sense, but as John pointed out, there's no ban on anything *inside* the uniform, and CTV rigged up Kate Pace with a wireless microphone transmitter under her jacket. At the same time, we fixed a camera far from the floor of the stadium that focussed exclusive-

ly on Kate and her reactions. Between microphone and camera, we hoped to get a personal and vibrant portrait of one Canadian athlete's up-close response to the glorious events. Kate seemed a logical choice since she's a bright, bubbly young woman who was, incidentally, coming up to her twenty-fifth birthday the very next day.

At first, the microphone yielded nothing except silence from Kate. She entered the stadium, and she was instantly spellbound by the grandeur of the setting. She said nothing, but her face, caught by the camera, told the story of the awe and joy she was feeling. As the athletes circled the stadium, Kate loosened up. In fact, she gave away her secret to the group of Canadians around her.

"I've got a mike pinned on me, you guys," Kate said.

*This page and next
The incredible jump-
ing of the Olympic
torch.*

Everybody leaned toward Kate and screamed in unison, "Hello Canada!"

"Can you believe that?" Kate said to freestyle skier, Katrina Kubenk. "Can you believe you just said hello to 27 million people?"

When the parade of athletes had finally taken their seats in the stadium, Juan Antonio Samaranch stepped to the microphone. Samaranch is a fellow who has attracted his share of controversy. In fact, a few days earlier, the legendary Norwegian cross-country skier Vegard Ulvang had openly criticized the International Olympic Committee in a television interview, particularly hammering Samaranch for his past ties with Spain's late fascist leader Francisco Franco. Ulvang's interview was a local sensation for days, though he and Samaranch later came to some accord. But nobody was

in a mood to challenge or speak ill of Samaranch on the night of the Opening Ceremony, not after the extraordinarily moving speech he offered his listeners in the stadium and on television.

Samaranch had just returned from Sarajevo. Poor, tragic, war-torn Sarajevo; ten years earlier, it had served as generous host to the Winter Games and the very stadium where those Games had seen their own Opening Ceremony had undergone an ugly metamorphosis. Now it was a cemetery. Samaranch, fresh from the site of this horrible reality, delivered the speech of his life. It was a tribute to the people of Sarajevo and it was a plea for peace.

"Please stop fighting. Please stop killing," he implored. "Drop your guns."

Then, as tears flowed down the cheeks of the members of the small team of competitors

from Bosnia, Samaranch called for a moment of silence.

This moving part of the Ceremony finally gave way to an explosion of a much different emotion, a rush of happy celebration, when Samaranch called on King Harald to speak the magic words.

"I declare open the Games of Lillehammer celebrating the Seventeenth Olympic Winter Games."

In all the jubilation that followed—the ovations, the marching-in of the Olympic flag, other activities—the highlight was, as always on these occasions, the lighting of the sacred Olympic flame. This has recently been pulled off with plenty of panache. Who can forget, for example, the archer at Barcelona firing a lighted arrow into the sky to launch the 1992 Summer Games? Norway had something equally spectacular

lined up for the Lillehammer Games, but, as it turned out, there had been a hitch along the way.

According to plan, cross-country skiers would carry the flame over the last leg of the long journey, crossing the Birkebeineren in relays. The last skier would reach the top of the Lysgaardsbakkene and pass on the torch to Norwegian ski jumping champ Ole Gunnar Fidjestol. Then Fidjestol—here's the real show-stopping part of the plan—would race down the ski jump, soar into space and make a gliding descent into the very bowl of the stadium, all the while holding the burning torch in one hand. On the drawing board, it looked like a thrilling piece of show business.

One problem, one very big problem: the morning before, Ole Gunnar Fidjestol, champion ski jumper, tried a practice run.

Maybe he put a little too much into the practice. Maybe he tried for just a touch too much show biz. The result was that he touched down, lost his balance, crashed into the snow and came out of the flight with a separated shoulder.

That accident brought, at the eleventh hour, a man named Stein Gruben to centre stage. He was the backup jumper, and it was up to him to replace the wounded Fidjestol and pull off the leap that was key to the entire ceremony of the flame.

In the best tradition of the old tale about the chorus girl replacing the lead singer just before the curtain goes up, Stein Gruben delivered the goods. He soared through the night air, torch flaming in one hand, and executed a perfect two-point landing. Kate Pace knew how beautifully Gruben had performed. From Kate's microphone, we could hear first

a gasp and then a scream of delight—at Gruben's sheer nerve.

Once on the ground, Gruben handed off the torch to Catherine Nottingnes. She was nineteen, a cross-country skier—and blind. Catherine passed the torch to Crown Prince Haakon, and it was his final task to climb the stairs to the Olympic cauldron and set it ablaze.

The Crown Prince made his climb, but for dramatic emphasis, at the top, he hesitated.

"Light it!" Kate Pace and the people around her yelled into her mike. "Light it!"

And he did. Flames burst upward in a wild dance of light. The snow that had been falling lightly throughout the Ceremony subsided. The clouds in the sky seemed to dissolve. There were no clouds, no falling snow, nothing except burning stars above us. The skies, though we didn't know it

then, would remain that way, clear and starry, for the rest of the Games.

The remainder of the Opening Ceremony rushed by in a colourful daze. There was the athletes' oath, the judges' oath, the playing and singing of the Norwegian anthem with 35,000 voices raised in patriotic song. Then the artistic program took over, an unbelievable show with reindeer, sleighs, skiers, singers, dancers, trolls emerging from the snow, haunting folk music and, lastly, fireworks.

"My cheeks," Kate Pace said into her microphone. "My cheeks are getting sore from smiling."

She wasn't the only one with that happy complaint.

DAY TWO

IT'S ALL IN THE GAMES

Sunday, February 13, 1994

In television, we have a cardinal rule. Actually we have a lot of cardinal rules, but this rule is more cardinal than some others: "Open big."

At these Games, the Canadian team "opened big." It chalked up a medal, a bronze, on the very first full day of competition. What added a bit more lustre to the achievement is that it came in the first high-profile medal event of the Games. This was the men's downhill run.

The fact is that the Canadian men's alpine team was long overdue to show some success in the Olympics. Plenty of resources and energy have gone into men's skiing, and with charismatic figures like the famed "Crazy Canucks," the skiers have often been in the limelight. All of which is fine and admirable, but in the past fourteen years of Olympic competition, these well-funded,

widely publicized skiers have won just a single Olympic medal.

The man who made a small but much-rejoiced change in that lamentable situation was Edi "Pod" Podivinsky. He nailed a bronze to double our Olympic medal total. It's a bit ironic that the other bronze medalist also bore the unusual nickname, Pod. Steve "Pod" Podborski won his at Lake Placid in 1980. He was one of Edi Podivinsky's heroes. Edi was 23, a former world junior champ, a guy who was full of promise and potential but also, a guy who was dogged by injuries. Maybe it didn't help Edi's progress that he could never say no to a good party. Or even to a bad party. He loved to eat junk food, and he loved to operate on the wild side, both in life and in skiing.

Then Podivinsky suffered the injury that made one injury too many as far as he was

Downhill
Alpine racing began late in the 1890s in Austria. Skiers used one long pole for balance and braking and followed a line straight down the hill with no turns or traverses. Gates were introduced in the 1920s. They are strategically placed along the course to reduce speed and mark the skier's path. The downhill event was introduced at the 1936 Olympics. There is only one objective: to get down the hill in the fastest time in the one allotted run.

concerned. It happened during a qualifying run for the 1992 Winter Olympics in Albertville. Pod crashed. He crashed so hard that he was out of the Games and into the hospital. That was where Edi saw the light. No more party animal for him, no more junk food, no more walks on the wild side. Instead, when he got back on his feet, he adhered to the same regimen followed by his teammate Cary Mullen: weight training in the gym, sensible diet at the training table, dedicated habits on the ski hills.

And at the Kvitfjell ski hill in Lillehammer shortly after eleven in the morning of Day Two of the Olympics, it all paid off for the Canadian with the new attitude. The weather was glorious, brilliant sunshine bathed the whole valley, and when Pod came out of the gate, he skied like a man possessed but, also, like a man in con-

trol. And the performance rewarded him with the bronze medal. Pod was third best on this day, at these Olympics, in the entire world.

In a crucial way, Podivinsky's triumph came as extremely welcome news to us on CTV. His bronze in the downhill meant that Valerie Pringle and I could sign on with big smiles and good news. It meant we could "open big."

Canada's hockey team opened in their event at the Games with a 7–2 win over Italy. In point of fact, you might say this was a win against an Italian-Canadian team since Italy was packed with players from Canada who enjoyed dual citizenship. For them, playing for Italy in the Olympics fulfilled a dream. As far as the Canadian team was concerned, the presence of all those players from back home in the Italian

sweaters meant that the game was marginally tougher than the team might have expected.

The Canadian team, as a matter of hard truth, carried a lot of baggage. Part of the baggage was historical; hockey is the game we're supposed to excel at—we do excel at it—but the last time Canada won an Olympic gold in the sport was 1952 when the Edmonton Mercurys represented us.

And part of the baggage was political; after all, for decades, Canada had been represented at the Games mostly by young amateurs and reinstated pros in the twilight of their careers while other countries, particularly Russia, were allowed to put their very best players on the ice, professional in fact if not in name.

With the collapse of the Iron Curtain, the tearing down of the Berlin Wall, the breakup of the Soviet Bloc, much had changed in the hockey world. Now the best Russian players were true pros playing in the NHL. That applied to a lesser extent to other Eastern teams. The balance of hockey power in the Olympics appeared to be shifting, though no one could be sure until the games were played out on the ice over the following two weeks.

One thing seemed absolutely certain: under any circumstances, the Canadian team would have a tough struggle to claim a medal at these Games. This wasn't essentially a team of professional stars. This was not even a team with a good pre-Olympic record. Through the winter months leading up to the Games, in exhibition matches in North America, Canada had been cuffed around fairly regularly by Team USA and by NHL teams. The situation didn't look

Tom Renney

93 CAN Peter Nedved

Trail Smoke-Eaters

The Trail Smoke-Eaters preceded their appearance at the 1961 World Championships in Geneva, Switzerland by a 3-month tour through Europe. They had played 51 games; they were tired when they showed up for the Championship but they were in peak condition. They tied the first game of the tournament with the Czechs. Both teams then went on to win all their games before meeting again in the final. The Smokies had to win by 4 goals to take the title. They won 5-1.

promising. That was an understatement. Team Canada's general-manager, George Kingston, speaking a couple of weeks before the Olympics began, said Canada would have to play better than they'd been able to so far, if they expected a shot at even a bronze medal.

But the team evolved. It had good hockey men at its helm. Tom Renney was the head coach, a no-nonsense British Columbian who grew up on glory tales of the Trail Smoke-Eaters winning the world championship for Canada in 1961. Renney's assistant, Dany Dubé, came out of the Québec Junior League. They shared one goal common to all winning coaches: they *hated* to lose.

Between the two of them, the coaches got the players thinking of concepts like team play, hard work, cohesion. And it helped

enormously that, in the last days leading up to the Games, terrific new players signed on board the Olympic team.

Petr Nedved was one. He was a marvelously inventive young player who had defected from his native Czechoslovakia when he was sixteen and playing in a midget tournament in Calgary. Now he had Canadian citizenship and, more to the point, now he was sitting out the NHL season in the salary dispute with the Vancouver Canucks. He offered his services to the Olympic Team. Who could turn him down?

Then there was Paul Kariya, a young man with impressive credentials. At the University of Maine, he led his team to the NCAA championship, won the Hobey Baker Award as the U.S. college player of the year, and came out of the NHL draft as

Yekaterina Gordeyeva & Sergei Grinkov

the first choice of the Anaheim Mighty Ducks and the fourth pick overall. This kid, a native of Vancouver, had the kind of play-making skills that made people whisper, ever so quietly, another Gretzky?

So Canada's team began to come together, a team that hadn't proved much yet, a team made up of players who had hung in from the start and others who were johnny-come-latelies, with names like Brian Savage, Todd Hlushko, Greg Johnson, Fabian Joseph, Chris Kontos, Adrian Aucoin, Dwayne Norris, Derek Mayer, goalie Corey Hirsch. Not exactly household names. And not a team that promised to have a lock on a medal. But it was a team that won its first game, beating Italy. And who knew what lay ahead?

The Olympic venues were hopping on the second day. At Hunderfossen, there was the men's single luge. There were other hockey games (Sweden threw a scare into the Russians before losing 5–1). And up on the Birkebeineren, it was the women's 15 km cross-country freestyle race. It was playing to huge crowds with hopes pinned on the local heroes, the Norwegian skiers, to tear up the course.

But that was nothing compared to what was going on in the Olympic Hall in Hamar, a town 45 km south of Lillehammer. It was, during the day, the venue for the 5000 m men's speedskating, and it was the place where a Norwegian named Johann Olav Koss was wrapping himself in glory. Koss won the 5000 m. He didn't just win it. He obliterated the competition and set a world record. The Norwegian crowd went wild. What they didn't know, what none of us knew, was that, for these Olympics, Koss was just warming up.

On an ordinary day, under normal conditions, I'm told the drive from Lillehammer to Hamar takes forty minutes, if you didn't stop for a cup of coffee. But on Day Two of the Olympics, late in the afternoon, the journey consumed at least an hour and a half. The road was clogged with buses and cars, and it seemed as if all the media people, who greatly outnumbered the 1884 athletes, were determined to make it to Hamar.

What was the big attraction?

The short program of the pairs figure skating. This was the stuff of potential high drama. This was a competition that matched up three pairs who ranked among the most dazzling of all time.

First, there was the Soviet pair of Ekaterina Gordeeva and Sergei Grinkov. They're a delightful couple, married, with a two-year-old daughter named Daria. Their reputation stemmed principally from the 1988 Calgary Olympics where they captured the gold. Then they turned pro. At the time, many knowledgeable people on the figure skating scene rated Gordeeva-Grinkov as the best ever. And it seemed to have occurred to Ekaterina and Sergei that maybe they had joined the professional ranks too early, that perhaps they should have given themselves more time for more gold medals. But it was impossible to turn back the clock until 1994 when, to everyone's astonishment, the Olympics were opened up to the pros. That brought Gordeeva and Grinkov rushing back.

The return of this veteran pair put them smack up against their successors, Artur Dmitriev and Natalia Mishkutenok. They were the Russian couple who won the gold at Albertville, the couple who had continued

their country's domination of pairs skating. It had been 34 years since a non-Soviet couple took the gold in pairs. That couple came from Canada, Barbara Wagner and Robert Paul and they were the winners at Squaw Valley in 1960.

The third pair who made this competition such a vivid contest were again Canadians who threatened the Soviets, Lloyd Eisler and Isabelle Brasseur. They had plenty to be proud of. They'd won the 1994 world's title in Prague, breaking a stranglehold that the Soviets had held on the championship since 1984 when yet another Canadian couple, Barbara Underhill and Paul Martini, had triumphed. Eisler and Brasseur had been on a hot streak over the previous year, beating everyone who tested them. The only couples they didn't defeat were the two who had been out of reach in the pros. Gordeeva-Grinkov

and Dmitriev-Mishkutenok. Finally at Lillehammer, all three couples, presumably at their peak, would meet in a winner-take-the-gold skateout.

Eisler and Brasseur are fascinating athletes. Lloyd is one hard competitor. That was obvious at Albertville. During Eisler-Brasseur's performance, Isabelle had taken a fall. It cost the couple at least one rung on the ladder, and they had to settle for the bronze. In the moments when Lloyd and Isabelle sat in the kiss-and-cry area where skaters wait to hear their final marks, Lloyd's anger, his disappointment, were palpable. He gave off discontent and dissatisfaction in waves that you could practically reach out and touch. That's the kind of competitor he is.

Underneath it all, though, under the tough exterior, Lloyd is actually a pussycat,

Hamar Olympic Amphitheatre
Also known as the Northern Lights Hall because of the enormous number of windows stylized to mirror the northern lights outside. This facility was home to both figure skating and short track speedskating. The building seats 6,000.

or, at least, Isabelle thinks so. She said before the Games, "I've been with Lloyd for seven years. We have our days, but most of the time, he's right there for me, trying to take care of me and make things easy for me. When I lost my dad, Lloyd was there the whole time, like a little boy trying to take away my pain."

Isabelle's father, Gilles, died just before the 1993 championships in Prague. Gilles was one of those ideal dads, supportive, a man who backed his daughter and her partner every step of the way. That was part of the reason for Isabelle's tears when *O Canada* played for the winners at Prague. Isabelle was thinking of her father at that moment of victory. So was Lloyd. These two make an authentic unit, bound together, and Prague represented a deserved peak for them.

Alas, as these Olympics drew near, it looked as if Lloyd and Isabelle would be up against horrendous odds in their attempt to duplicate Prague. At a practice session just before the Games began, the two were working on one of the tosses that highlight their performances. The lifts and throws that these two build into their routine are totally dynamic. But this time, in practice, Isabelle crashed through Lloyd's catch and slammed into his shoulder. She took the blow in the chest, and when the doctors checked her over, the news was all bad: a cracked rib for Isabelle.

On the night of Day Two, in the Olympic Amphitheatre for the pairs short program, the three principal couples skated in the last grouping.

First up were Eisler and Brasseur. Almost from the opening seconds, it was clear that Isabelle was in terrible pain. Her rib must

have been throbbing, and, as far as the judges were concerned, the Eisler-Brasseur program didn't quite cut it. The marks weren't terrible. In fact, under the circumstances, they were good. But the judges left plenty of room for the other two pairs to catch and pass them.

Gordeeva and Grinkov, next up, seemed to be uncharacteristically nervous, especially Sergei. Maybe it was all those years away from competition that rattled them. But they quickly settled into it, and the two of them, led by Ekaterina, soon had the judges and the crowd in the palms of their hands.

Dmitriev and Mishkutenok finished off the evening, and they were in stellar form. But it wasn't good enough to wipe away the memory left by Gordeeva and Grinkov, and when the marks were totalled, Sergei and Ekaterina held top spot. Dmitriev and Mishkutenok stood second—a placing that drew a look of total disgust from Artur Dmitriev—and that left Canada's best, the gallant, and wounded, Brasseur and Eisler looking up from third place, looking ahead to the free skate in forty-eight hours.

DAY THREE

HEARTS AND HEARTBREAK

Monday, February 14, 1994

Did anyone, amid all the Olympic madness, notice that it was Valentine's Day?

Practically the entire world.

When we arrived at the International Broadcast Centre early on the morning of Day Three, the studio was filled with flowers and best wishes. They came from fans, athletes, fellow workers, and from just plain friends.

And there were cards and E-mail messages. Electronic mail has become a popular form of communication at recent Olympic Games. Friends have been made, hearts have been won, battles have been fought, all on the E-mail. The part that touched me, particularly, were the messages from athletes. Isabelle Brasseur sent one to my colleague, Dave Toms, one of our Olympic writers who excelled on the E-mail. I would have thought she'd have too much on her mind, too much concern and pain to remember

others. But that's Isabelle, an extraordinarily thoughtful woman.

In her note, Isabelle wrote of her sweetheart, Jean-Luc Brassard. Isabelle's thoughts were with Brassard because he, like her, is an athlete, and just as she was, he was going for the gold. Jean-Luc is a world champion skier on the mogul hills. He said that the night before, in the arena over in Hamar, looking down at Isabelle skating and fighting back pain, he was more nervous watching her compete in her sport than he was competing in *his*. Isabelle's turn to watch Jean-Luc would come on Day Five.

The single men's luge event was held on this day. Only one Canadian competed: Clay Ives finished 20th. If you're wondering how and why he got the urge to become a human bullet on a roller coaster of ice, ask Clay's parents. They built a natural mini-luge run in

Birkebeineren Ski Stadium
Birkebeineren is the spectacular home to cross-country skiing, biathlon and Nordic combined cross-country. The capacity of the stadium is 25,000; tens of thousands more people line the actual ski trails.

their backyard in Bancroft, Ontario. The *naturbahn* track became—predictably!–popular with the neighbourhood kids and it also helped Clay get hooked on the sport at a young age. Clay still had one big event to look forward to, the men's double luge in four days, where he and his teammate Bob Casper would make their final run as a team.

The Norwegians, I was beginning to understand, are a funny, wry people. Quite a contrast from their reputation as being shy and dour. There's a joke they like to tell on themselves. It's about the first conversation between two Norwegians. The first, an elder, had lived alone for years at the end of a northern fjord. One day the elder ventured out of the fjord to the top of a nearby mountain. Across the valley, he spotted another man for the first time. Reacting to his first contact with another person in decades, the

elder cupped his hands to his mouth and shouted to the distant stranger, "Go away!"

The point of the joke—this is something else I came to understand—is that the Norwegians are just the opposite of the elder. They aren't cold and standoffish. They are friendly and approachable.

They're also proud to an almost ferocious degree, and on Day Three they had plenty of opportunity to put their pride on display.

The first place where the Norwegians whooped it up was at the Birkebeineren. The event was the men's 30 km free technique cross-country ski race. At least 100,000 spectators lined the route that the race followed, and they went unabashedly crazy with excitement. That was because not one Norwegian but two dominated the race. The two were Thomas Alsgaard and Bjorn Daehlie, and they ran one-two through a gauntlet of their

fellow countrymen and countrywomen who sent up the wildest racket I've ever heard. There were ringing cowbells, screams, whoops, cheers and the totally unique cry that sounds like oy-oy-oy-oy. And all that cheering paid off because the two local heroes maintained their one-two placing to the very end, bringing a gold to Alsgaard and a silver to Daehlie.

The second venue where the Norwegians celebrated on Day Three was on Kvitfjell where the men were competing in the combined downhill and where Lasse Kjus took the gold for Norway. Canadians had good reason to feel pounding hearts in this event because we had two skiers who did us proud. The first was Edi Podivinsky who had streaked his way to the downhill bronze on Day One, and here he was, two days later, finishing a creditable fifth in the combined downhill. The other was Cary Mullen.

Cary is a true Albertan. In the summer, he lives on the family farm in the country between Calgary and Banff. But as soon as the first snow flies, he heads into the mountains and spends the entire winter on skis. As a young boy, he drew his inspiration from the success of Canada's Crazy Canucks.

"I vividly remember the 1980 Olympics at Lake Placid," he told me. "I remember watching Ken Read and watching Steve Podborski win his bronze. I remember the adrenalin I felt back then, and I knew I wanted to be up there myself some day."

In Lillehammer, Cary almost realized his ambition. He whipped himself down the hill in a great run. His time was among the best of the day. But Lasse Kjus, the Norwegian gold medalist, finished ahead of him. So did two Americans, Kyle Rasmussen and Tommy Moe, who took the silver and

29

Speedskating

Speedskating competitions were recorded in the Netherlands during the 13th century; the first organized race was reputed to have been held in England in 1763. Speedskating is one of the original Winter Olympic events and as such, dates back to 1924.

In long track skaters race counterclockwise, in pairs, on two lanes of a 400 m oval track. It is a timed race; fastest wins.

bronze. Next came Cary, in fourth place and out of the medals by the most heartbreaking of margins.

But the real heartbreak of Day Three belonged to a man who, sadly, had become no stranger to tragedy and disappointment. This was Dan Jansen of the United States.

The Jansen saga began at the 1988 Games in Calgary. He ranked as a favourite in the speedskating sprints, but he went into the Games knowing that his beloved sister Jane was in the terminal stages of leukemia. Then, on the very day of Dan's 500 m race, Jane died. Dan, desperate to win for his sister, dedicated the race to her. But fate played Dan a terrible trick—he came down in a crashing fall in the 500 and won no medal.

Nor was fate finished with Dan Jansen. In the 1000 m, which he again dedicated to Jane, he fell once more, and it was the slow-motion image of Dan, caught on television, sliding helplessly into the crash barrier that has stuck with millions of people as the very definition of despair.

Now, in 1994, Dan was back on Day Three of these Olympics to lay claim to a medal. The event was the 500 m. Again Dan was the favourite. Again he had dedicated the race to Jane. But this Jane was his baby daughter. Dan's wife Robin had given birth to the little girl in late 1993, and the couple had named her after Dan's late sister. It seemed at last time for Dan Jansen to win a break from fate and take home the gold.

It wasn't to be. Dan didn't fall this time. He "bobbled." It was no more than a slip of his blade that brought the briefest touch of his hand against the ice. But in the flying pace of the 500 m, it takes only the tiniest

error to throw a skater off pace. It was enough to cost Dan his medal. For Dan Jansen, it was despair revisited. Maybe, like so many other great athletes, his dream of gold would go unanswered. On this day he was again out of the medals, in eighth place. His very last shot at a medal would come in four days.

Sylvain Bouchard of Loretteville, Québec led the Canadian brigade. He finished three places behind Jansen in 11th, Patrick Kelly of Toronto was 12th and the Ireland brothers from Winnipeg, Sean and Mike, ended up in 17th and 26th respectively.

Hamar Olympic Hall
The venue for long track speedskating. The Hall looks like an inverted Viking Ship with a centre beam than runs like a keel from one end to the other. Located on the shores of Lake Mjosa; it seats 10,500.

DAY FOUR

A LITTLE LIGHT IN HAMAR

Tuesday, February 15, 1994

Facing page
Kerrin-Lee Gartner
skis the Super G at
Kvitjell.

I got to work at the International Broadcast Centre early in the morning and found that everyone was thinking about Isabelle Brasseur and Lloyd Eisler. That night, they'd be skating in the pairs long program. Would Isabelle's cracked rib hold up to the demands of the competition? Would she and Lloyd skate the performance of their dreams? Would they overtake the two great Russian couples? Would they win gold? The tension was terrific, but the pairs event was hours away, and in the meantime, there were other sports to cover, other champions to report.

For starters, there was the women's Super G alpine event out at Kvitfjell. Canada had three skiers in that one who rated a solid chance for a medal.

One was Michelle Ruthven. She was Michelle McKendry before her marriage, and under that name, she'd been an Olympian at both Calgary and Albertville. More to the point, Michelle had been ripping up the circuit on the World Cup through the early part of this season.

Then there was the marvelous Kerrin-Lee Gartner. There was one worry about Kerrin-Lee. She had been devastated by the death of her friend Ulrike Maier of Austria a few weeks before the Games. Ulrike had been killed in a racing accident, and there had been talk that Kerrin-Lee, still deeply in mourning, might drop out of competition. But at race time, Kerrin-Lee, the gold medalist of the Albertville Games, showed up, in grief perhaps but ready to race.

The third member of the Canadian trio was CTV's star of the Opening Ceremony, Kate Pace. Kate had had this race to look forward to since winning on this course in a

Hafjell
The venue for the slalom and giant slalom events with a capacity of 22,000. The women's downhill event was moved from this location to the men's course at Kvitfjell after several racers protested that the Hafjell course was too easy.

Super G
The Super G course is somewhere between that of Downhill and Giant Slalom: the vertical drop is almost as great as Downhill and the number of gates are fewer than Slalom or Giant Slalom. In the women's race, the vertical drop is between 400-600m with at least 30 gates. For men, the vertical drop is 500-650 m, with at least 35 gates. Karen Percy took bronze in this event at Calgary.

pre-Olympic competition the year before. Kate, of North Bay, Ontario, was coming into her own as the reigning world downhill champion and the most consistent skier on the tour. She deserved every success that came her way. She'd worked for it. Early in her career, injuries had practically cancelled her chances at medal placings. But hard work and tough-mindedness got her back on track.

It's altogether typical of Kate and her attitude that she adheres to a special motto. It goes: "If I don't train hard today, someone else will." Those words are taped to the handle bars of the bike that Kate rides around her home town for dry land training. And then there's the absolutely unique gimmick Kate employs to keep her confidence level up. It centres on a sort of mental treasure box. Kate puts it this way: "I

built something in my head, a treasure box. And in it, I put all my favourite things, my favourite places, favourite music, all the good qualities about myself. Then, on those days when the real confidence isn't there for me, I lift up the lid of my treasure box and let the good things flow out. That helps me believe in who I am and what I'm trying to achieve."

Unfortunately for Kate and for Canada, the treasure box would not include a medal from the Super G. She finished twelfth in a race that saw an American, Diann Roffe-Steinrotter, take gold. Michelle Ruthven was twenty-fifth, and Kerrin-Lee Gartner did best of the Canadians, taking eighth place. The glamour event, the downhill, was still to come.

There were good things in the hockey arena for Canada on Day Four. Bizarre but

34

good. Canada played France in the second game for both teams. The French team, propped up by a few imports of the dual citizenship variety from Canada, had a mere ten shots on Corey Hirsch in the Canadian net. One of the shots made it into the net. Canada, on the other hand, managed 35 shots but scored just three goals.

Actually, it was one Canadian player who did all of the crucial shooting and scoring. He was Todd Hlushko. Todd came to the Games with a touching personal history. His father had died in the summer of 1993, just a few months earlier, and before he died, Mr. Hlushko told Todd to go to Lillehammer and bring back a gold medal for Canada. Todd took those words and the mission to heart, and in the game against France he pumped in two goals including the winner. Another Todd, Todd Warriner,

netted the third Canadian goal. Canada was 2–and–0 leading Pool B.

The surprise result of the day came from the American's game against Slovakia in Gjøvik's Ice Cavern. A tie! People were starting to like the Slovakian's spirited style. They attacked every shift as though it might be their last and their games provided some of the most entertaining hockey of the round robin section of the tournament.

Maybe the best story of Day Four—apart from whatever Lloyd Eisler and Isabelle Brasseur were saving up for that night in the pairs—belonged to the remarkable Lyubov Egorova. She's a Russian cross-country skier, and she came into the Games already the winner of three gold medals and two silvers at the Albertville Olympics. Her ambition was to capture at least five more medals at Lillehammer. That would tie her

Gjøvik Olympic Cavern Hall
One of the two venues for hockey, Gjøvik is a 10,000 square metre, 5,500 seat arena that is burrowed 120 metres into the heart of a mountain. The building is an engineering marvel. Its rock walls are sprayed with a layer of charcoal-covered cement, to spectacular effect.

Birkebeineren Ski Stadium

60 RUS Ljubov Egorova

Cross-country skiing

Cross-country has been on the Olympic program since 1924. Its roots lie in Norway when, in 1206, an infant royal son was carried to safety over the mountains by two "Birkebeiner" scouts. The Birkebeinerrennet race is held annually in Norway to commemorate this occasion. The terrain of a race course is divided, more or less, equally between up hill, down hill and rolling sections. Skiers start at 30-second intervals in individual races and in a mass start for relay events. Races are designated as either classic for which the skiers must use the diagonal stride, or free technique where skiers ski-skate.

with her former teammate, Raisa Smetanina, who had won an amazing ten medals in her Olympic career. What was even more astounding about Smetanina was that, at Albertville, winning the last of her haul of medals, she was 40 years old, the oldest woman athlete to win a medal of any sort in Winter Games history. And now Lyubov Egorova had set herself the target of matching Smetanina's record of ten overall Olympic medals.

Egorova had got off to a super start on Day Two by taking the silver in her first race, the 15 km freestyle. The gold went to the woman who would turn out to be Egorova's great rival in these Games. She was Italy's Manuela Di Centa, and on Day Four, in the 5 km classic, the two competitors again went head to head. Another skiing superstar, Marja-Liisa Kirvesniemi, the star of Sarajevo in 1984, had

returned to competition after starting a family. This race was truly a battle of cross-country ski titans.

This time, Egorova triumphed in a magnificent race. She took gold, Di Centa settled for silver and Kirvesniemi of Finland, the bronze. Egorova's medal count was up to seven with more races to come.

Once again, the road to Hamar was jammed in the late afternoon. Nobody wanted to miss the climax to the thrilling pairs competition. Gordeeva-Grinkov, Dmitriev-Mishkutenok, Eisler-Brasseur. Who would take the gold? The odds were against the Canadians, in third place and flying on one wing, but if they delivered a flawless performance and both of the Russian pairs faltered, then gold wasn't out of the question.

Eisler said before the Games "I think we're going to Lillehammer to put a performance

down there that can give us a gold medal. Even if it doesn't give us a gold medal and we still have that performance, we'll still be happy. I mean if they beat us because they skate better, more power to them. I'm going to be happy because I know that we got beaten on our best day. In Lillehammer we're going to give it our best shot."

Isabelle saw it in a similar light, "We got bronze in Albertville. Silver and gold at Worlds. I mean we've got all the colours. So we're just going out there and if we get silver, great. If we get another bronze, great. As long as we skate well and come off the ice and feel good. That's all we want."

We had two voices of experience to describe the unfolding of tonight's events to our viewers back home. One of our commentators was former world champion Brian Orser, the man who'd won silver in

the men's singles not once but twice, at the Calgary Olympics and at the Albertville Games. And our second expert was another silver medalist, Debbi Wilkes, who, with her partner Guy Revell, had won the pairs silver at the Innsbruck Olympics in 1964.

From our broadcast area, we had only to glance behind and to the left to take in the Canadian contingent of supporters for Lloyd and Isabelle. The entire Canadian skating team had turned out, Kurt Browning in the middle, Elvis Stojko beside him, and others spread across the rows, Josée Chouinard, Susan Humphreys, Victor Kraatz, Shae-Lynn Bourne. Lloyd's father was there, Lloyd Sr., wearing his trademark black stetson, as was Lloyd's mom, Bev. So was Isabelle's mother, Claudette. The whole gang radiated nerves and anxiety, but they made for a great cheering section.

Other Pairs
Canada's other pairs teams, those still working their way up the ladder, did well. Jamie Salé and Jason Turner wound up 12th and Kristy Sargeant and Kris Wirtz took the 10th spot.

As in the short program two nights earlier, the three contending pairs came on at the end of the evening. Lloyd and Isabelle skated first. Given the pressure they were under, given Isabelle's cracked rib, they were nothing short of magnificent. Their tosses worked to a degree that approached perfection. And their lifts were thrilling enough to bring the audience to warm, noisy appreciation.

But was something missing?

Debbi Wilkes probably put her finger on the absent factor when she explained that the one flaw in the Eisler-Brasseur performance was a lack of sustained speed. The Russians, she reckoned, would move faster.

The judges must have agreed with Debbi because they marked Lloyd and Isabelle in the 5.7 range, solid but probably not good enough to edge out either of the Russian pairs.

And that's the way the competition unfolded. Dmitriev and Mishkutenok moved beautifully across the ice, genuine visions on ice. They outscored Lloyd and Isabelle, but as it turned out, their marks and their artistry were eclipsed by Gordeeva and Grinkov who seemed to draw inspiration from the challenge of their Russian teammates. So, in the end, it was gold for Gordeeva-Grinkov, silver for Dmitriev-Mishkutenok, and bronze for Eisler-Brasseur.

Yekaterina was emotional when she spoke about winning another gold medal. "It's different this time," she said with moist eyes. "In Calgary, we were so young we couldn't enjoy it. This time we win for our daughter and for our new country."

Brasseur and Eisler were emotional too. This was their last Olympic free skate

before turning professional and they weren't going away disappointed. They were happy with their performance just like they wanted to be. They skated as well as they could and Lloyd told a national television audience, "Hey, we did our best and I don't [care] if people are disappointed that we didn't win gold. We did our best."

But, in a curious twist, it may have been Lloyd and Isabelle whom the crowd would remember when they left the arena. Lloyd ensured that. When the couple were called onto the ice to receive their bronze medals, Lloyd, breaking with Olympic tradition, picked up Isabelle, perched her on his shoulder and performed a gorgeous spin. It was a moment of wit and grace and humour—and entirely unforgettable.

DAY FIVE

FLYING WITHOUT WINGS

Wednesday, February 16, 1994

To many, Jean-Luc Brassard qualifies as a hero. That isn't a word to toss around lightly, not in this slightly jaundiced age.

Jean-Luc possesses all the right personal qualities, charm, kindness, generosity. And then—here's where he's elevated to heroic status—he has unbelievable courage. He needs it. After all, he's a freestyle skier. He takes part in a sport that demands style, grace, speed and huge amounts of daring. It's a sport for heroes. Jean-Luc is the genuine article.

Jean-Luc grew up in an elegant two-storey house on Grand-Ile along the banks of the St. Lawrence River between Montreal and Cornwall. It's a lovely spot with a big yard, plenty of apple trees, and a back lawn that slopes down to a retaining wall at the edge of the St. Lawrence. Jean-Luc's father is a retired teacher, his mother a practising teacher, and his sister, Anne-Marie, a designer and manufacturer of ski wear. In fact, it was Anne-Marie who designed the Canadian Air Force freestyle jackets that Jean-Luc wears so proudly.

Jean-Luc's inspiration to get into his unlikely sport came via television. As a little kid, he was rivetted by the televised antics of two pioneer members of the freestyle skiing fraternity, the brothers Yves and Dom LaRoche of the Québec Air Force. Jean-Luc watched the LaRoches spinning off snow-covered bumps, soaring at breakneck speeds, tumbling and rocketing through the air. And he knew that somehow he had to get in on this amazing and acrobatic sport.

That was a tall order for a kid living on the banks of the St. Lawrence far from the mountains and moguls of Québec. But the young Jean-Luc was a resourceful boy, and

Moguls Event

Moguls received full medal status for the Albertville Olympics. Skiers face a steep—up to 32 degree—course that is between 200 and 270 m long and covered with bumps. They are scored by judges on their technical turning ability and strong, aggressive fall-line skiing. The speed in which they ski the course also forms part of their total score. Two jumps must be performed during each run. Height and distance, form and precision and clean landings are all part of the equation in the judges' marks.

he fashioned his own daredevil landscape. He began early one winter by dragging his dad's ladder out of the garage and lashing it against the eavestrough over the family room of the Brassard house. Then he laid boards and blankets over the spaces between the ladder's rungs and hosed the whole apparatus with water that froze instantly. "What I had," Jean-Luc recalls, "was something like a backyard rink on a steep angle." He packed snow over the track at the foot of the ladder, and, *voilà*, a home-made freestyle platform.

Brassard family snapshots preserve what happened next on this contraption. The pictures show Jean-Luc standing at the top of the ladder. They show him flying through the air. They show him making two-point landings. And they show him braking fiercely at the retaining wall beside the St.

Lawrence. In all the photos, Jean-Luc wears a broad, brave smile. Jean-Luc's father gave him a nickname: Wonderboy. Jean-Luc lived by one motto: "I love to fly."

Jean-Luc wasn't far into his teens when he was flying on the real freestyle skiing circuit. And in no time, in a remarkably short time, by 1992, he reigned as the champion of the world in his sport.

The one blip on his progress came at the Albertville Olympics when freestyle skiing was first admitted as an Olympic sport. Jean-Luc, all of nineteen years old, thought he was prepared for the Games. Maybe he was in physical terms, but as it developed, in mental terms, he still had a lesson or two to absorb.

The man who taught him was Edgar Grospiron of France. Grospiron ranked as one of the wild men of the sport, the guy they called "Crazy Eddy." In Albertville, in

Facing page
Jean-Luc Brassard
after winning gold
in the moguls event.

front of his own countrymen, Grospiron was in no mood to concede the gold medal. And he didn't. He absolutely devoured the moguls hills on the course at Tignes, and in the final, he recorded the fastest time and won from the judges the second highest marks for turns and air. His overall points total confirmed him as the gold medalist.

As for Jean-Luc, he settled for seventh place, but he looked on the positive side of the Olympic experience. He said he learned from his loss. "When I took my position in the starting gate," he said later, "all I could see were the red lights on the cameras pointing at me. I could hear the people clapping, and I was thinking, whew, it's time to put on a show. But I think I tried too hard that morning. I think I got too intense. And at the bottom, after it was over, I knew I could have done much better."

In the next two years, he did a whole lot better. He emerged as the darling of the moguls circuit. He knocked Crazy Eddy Grospiron off the throne and redefined the entire notion of freestyle champion. He never lost his modesty or his graciousness; Jean-Luc was undoubtedly the stuff that champs are made of.

That was the period, 1992, when Jean-Luc also found romance. He met Isabelle Brasseur, and love was in the air. It was a rough period for Isabelle in her family life and her professional life. In January, her grandfather died. In February, she fell at Albertville, probably costing the Eisler-Brasseur pair a medal higher than bronze. In March, the couple again came up short at the world championships. And in the autumn, Isabelle's father, Gilles, passed away. Lloyd Eisler supported Isabelle through her grief. And so did Jean-Luc.

Edgar Grospiron
After winning gold at Albertville, Edgar "Crazy Eddy" Grospiron was asked if he had a special diet while training. His answer, designed to confirm his reputation, was, "Yes, one week red wine and the next week, white."

Jean-Luc Brassard
"I felt a lot of pressure while I was on top," Brassard said after his gold medal run. "I was just going to go down the hill as a robot. I didn't know I had won until I looked up at the scoreboard. When I did, it was the greatest day, greatest moment of my life."

On Day Five at Lillehammer, Jean-Luc's career was positioned to move up to the next level, to gold medal status. As he waited to make his run, he knew exactly what was needed. Crazy Eddy Grospiron had taken his run. Amazingly, he stood second at that point. He wouldn't be winning a second gold medal in moguls. The surprise leader, the man Jean-Luc had to beat, was the Russian Sergei Shupletsov who had racked up an impressive point total of 26.90. Jean-Luc steeled himself.

It was a near miraculous run. On the second jump, he performed the Iron Cross-Cossack combination that he'd made his speciality. This time, he pulled it off without a hitch. He put all the rest of his talents on vivid display—the speed and the balletic grace, while he pumped his knees like shock absorbers, over and over. The run consumed all of 24.5 seconds, and at the bottom Jean-Luc shook his fists at the heavens in glee.

Would the judges agree that Jean-Luc had triumphed?

Yes, they would. They awarded Jean-Luc 27.24 points. That meant first place. That meant a gold medal, Canada's first of the Games, a gold for a new hero.

Speaking of heroes, Norway's was still at it. This was the mighty Johann Olav Koss. Three days earlier, he had taken the gold in the men's 5000 m speedskating. And now, on Day Five, he upped the ante with another gold, this time in the 1500 m which he won in Olympic-record time.

The Norwegians loved this man, and it was small wonder. At the Albertville Games, he had been practically crippled when he passed a gallstone on the day of the

Opening Ceremony. Still, he insisted on racing, and only eight days after being in the hospital he took gold in the 1500 m and silver in the 10 000 m.

Koss, a 25-year-old medical student, was all heart, all generosity. At Lillehammer, he donated the $40,000, which his sponsors had put up for winning a gold medal, to the Olympic Aid Project that benefitted people living in Sarajevo's war zone.

Johann Olav Koss was, like Jean-Luc Brassard, all hero.

DAY SIX

*Facing page
Kurt Browning,
four-time world
champ, after his
short program.*

ICE WARS

Thursday, February 17, 1994

The day began, slightly ridiculously, in anticlimax.

Tonya Harding had arrived in Lillehammer. So had Nancy Kerrigan. Both were lined up for practice sessions. By a quirk in scheduling, the two were timed to practice on the same ice surface at the same time.

The media swarmed.

All of us watched. Cameras were poised. Tape recorders and pencils were set to record the fateful events, to take note of whatever words were spoken at this grand encounter.

And what did we draw?

A gigantic, yawning blank. Nothing happened. Harding skated. Kerrigan skated. And neither looked at the other or had anything to say to the other.

After this fiasco, we all wondered: which was sillier, the Harding-Kerrigan story or the coverage it was generating?

Meanwhile, at other venues in the Olympic area, many competing athletes were generating much real news.

Lyubov Egorova was still single-mindedly at it. She was the Russian cross-country skier who was attempting to bring her list of Olympic medals to a record ten. She started at the Lillehammer Games with five career medals; then she took silver on Day Two and gold on Day Four and on this day, captured another gold in the 10 km freestyle pursuit. That made eight medals and still counting. Again her closest competitor was Manuela Di Centa, who finished just seconds behind for the silver, with another Italian, Stepahania Belmondo, taking bronze.

It was a good day for Russia. At the Viking Ship speedskating venue, Russian skater, Svetlana Bazanova, took a surprise

*This page and next
Bjorn Daehlie of
Norway finishing the
10 km classic race.*

Svetlana Bazanova
Speedskater Svetlana
Bazanova philoso-
phized about her gold
medal win against
Gunda Niemann, "I
believe (Niemann) was
the most probable win-
ner at this distance, but
people fall. That's life."

gold in the women's 3000 m. Before the race, Gunda Niemann of Germany, the defending champion and world record holder, seemed to have a lock on the 3000. But Niemann fell on the very curve that earlier had cost Dan Jansen his chance at a medal and she was disqualified. Niemann didn't just slip, as Jansen had—she clipped a lane marker and crashed to the ice. A tragedy for Niemann, a gold medal for Bazanova.

Over at the Birkebeineren Stadium, the Norwegians were setting off their familiar cry of oy-oy-oy-oy. The centre of all the jubilation was, once again, the cross-country skier, Bjorn Daehlie. It may be difficult to grasp this concept in North America, but in Norway, Daehlie and his compatriot, Vegard Ulvang, are to cross-country skiing what Gretzky and Lemieux are to hockey in Canada. These guys are superstars and mil-

lionaires. Between the two of them, they had won three golds and a silver at Albertville. The Norwegians worshipped them and made them rich men.

Now, at Lillehammer, Ulvang seemed to be slipping. Maybe his concentration was off; his brother had gone on a cross-country ski expedition some months before and had never come back. In the men's classic 10 km race at Lillehammer, in an event that was once Ulvang's speciality, he struggled to seventh place. This was a man who had, in his short lifetime to date, scaled Mt. McKinley, skied across Greenland, and conducted an Olympic peace-keeping mission to Sarajevo. They called him the "Viking" in Norway, but he seemed to be falling away from his former greatness. Never mind, on this day, Day 6, his teammate, Bjorn Daehlie, won the gold in the 10 km. Oy-oy-oy-oy.

On the ski hills at Kvitfjell, it was a great day for the Americans. Specifically for Tommy Moe in the men's Super G. It was Moe's twenty-fourth birthday, and the 60,000 fans watching the event serenaded him with a rousing rendition of Happy Birthday. Moe responded by racing to a silver medal. The German veteran, Markus Wasmeier, took gold, while the Norwegian, Kjetil Andre Aamodt, won the bronze. In this race Canada had no reason to celebrate with standings of 24th (Cary Mullen), 27th (Brian Stemmle) and Did Not Finish (Edi Podivinsky and Ralf Socher).

Canada had partial reason for satisfaction on the hockey ice at Hakan Hall in Lillehammer. Our team went into the game with a 2–0 record while its opponent, the United States, showed two ties. At the end of the contest, the U.S. string was intact with yet another tie. That wasn't the only statistic that made the game unique. This was also a game in which Canada was awarded two penalty shots. Petr Nedved converted on one, Greg Johnson missed on the second. Dwayne Norris connected for the other two Canadian goals. And, if nothing else, the tie kept Canada in the category of unbeaten teams. The Americans were, if anything, consistent—3 straight ties.

But the big action of Day Six was scheduled for the evening at the Olympic Amphitheatre in Hamar. This was the battle of champions, the great male figure skaters of the world, pro and amateur, coming together to fight it out for Olympic gold, beginning, on this night, with the short program.

Kurt Browning was here, a four-time world's champ, the reigning world title-holder, but never an Olympic gold medalist.

*Facing page
Elvis Stojko competing
in the men's short
program*

*This page
Two great Canadians—
Elvis Stojko and Kurt
Browning*

"This time of my life quite possibly will never be duplicated again," he said before he performed. "The excitement, the pressure, the expectations. Stepping out on the ice and knowing the whole world is watching. If I can just make everybody remember something. Give them something so they won't forget."

Brian Boitano was back too, the gold medalist at Calgary, world professional champ, returning to see if he still had the stuff for another gold.

Viktor Petrenko had the same thoughts. He'd won gold at the Albertville Olympics. Could he duplicate that triumph of two years earlier? Aleksei Urmanov, Russian champion and world bronze medalist, Scott Davis, the U.S. champion, Philippe Candeloro, France's flamboyant champ, second in Europe, fifth in the worlds, all carried the same hopes for glory.

This promised to be a shootout, and one guy with plenty of firepower, a skater from the new generation, was Canada's own Elvis Stojko. We knew he was a tremendously athletic and exhilarating performer. We knew he was coming in on a high after defeating Kurt Browning in the Canadian championships. But what about the Olympics? Could Elvis, competing against all the returning pros, these legends of artistry, meet the toughest challenge of all? Stojko did not appear concerned. "If two Canadian flags get up on the podium, I think it will be the biggest thing that has ever happened in figure skating. You know, Kurt and I do our own things as individuals and we compete hard against each other but in the end I hope we're gonna be up there together. That would make it perfect."

Oddly enough at 7 o'clock that night, the Amphitheatre was only half full, people still

streaming in from the cold, when the first skater stepped on to the ice. What was even odder was that the first skater was none other than Brian Boitano. Was this any way to treat a former gold medalist? Was it fair to make him skate in the dreaded first position? Maybe not, but it was the luck of the draw. Reinstated pros were required to draw for one of the opening twelve placements in the technical program. Boitano picked number one. Bad luck, but then it was Boitano who had said earlier, "People ask me if it's a risk going back to the Olympics. I tell them I'm compelled to take the risk, that I have no choice. I hate the thought of lying on my death bed when I'm, say, 93, and being filled with regret for not having tried."

Those were courageous words. Boitano couldn't deliver on them. He looked tentative during his loosening-up skate. A few

moments later, as he got into his program, he looked lost. He fell on the triple Axel. He couldn't complete the required combination. Everything went wrong, and at the end of the evening, Brian Boitano would be placed a humiliating eighth. The only comfort he could take, if comfort it was, was that another former gold medalist, Viktor Petrenko, did worse. After his skate, he would stand in ninth place.

With the old pros tumbling all around—literally, physically tumbling—the young skaters tried to seize the chance for a breakthrough. Great Britain's Steven Cousins, for one, put on the show of his life. Cousins acquired a Canadian connection in the months before the Olympics when he trained alongside Elvis Stojko with coach, Doug Leigh. In the Amphitheatre in Hamar, you could see Cousins' eyes light up after his

performance. He knew he'd done the job, and at the end of the evening, he would stand in seventh place. That was three places up on another promising youngster, Canada's Sébastien Britten. It was Sébastien's first Olympics. Like many first-time competitors, he felt overwhelmed by the experience. Skating as efficiently as he did, with such speed and finesse—that was a bonus.

Next up was Elvis. He was young but hardly a raw rookie. After all, he'd skated for Canada at Albertville where he finished seventh. His fans insisted he deserved better, that the judges hadn't appreciated his brand of modern, athletic artistry. But, never mind, Lillehammer was a whole new ball game, and this was a more confident Elvis. On the ice, immediately before he went into his routine, Elvis was an absolute study in concentration. Then he exploded into his moves. He tore up the ice, nailing every jump, corkscrewing every spin. He couldn't be denied, and the judges placed him in first place on the leader board.

The next couple of skaters took their shots. The U.S.'s Scott Davis, the best spinner among the men, didn't quite produce the goods. He finished fourth. Russia's Oleg Tataurov, competent and pleasing, was one place back in fifth. But another Russian, Aleksei Urmanov, was something different, something special. Where Elvis was rock'n'roll, Urmanov was ballet. To be sure, he had his own brand of steel, and even though extravagant costumes and an elaborate style were his hallmarks, Urmanov could jump with the best. He produced the jumps on this night. He even landed a triple Axel/double toe combination that wowed the crowd. The judges were

Figure Skating
Competitive skating began in the 1800s though it wasn't until 1907 that a world championship was held in which both women and men competed. Judges mark the technical, or short, program for required elements and presentation; they mark the free skate, or long program, for technical merit and artistic impression. Marks are deducted from skaters if they omit a required element or fail in their attempt to perform that element.

*This page and next
Kurt Browning's short
program and his dis-
appointment*

impressed by the way the young man—Urmanov is only twenty—brought together all the elements in one essentially classic package, and they awarded him marks that vaulted Urmanov over Stojko into first place on the board.

Two skaters were left. France's Philippe Candeloro was one. He's a natural showman on ice, and he put plenty of his usual dazzle into his performance in the Amphitheatre. The judges rewarded him with third place, a nice present for Candeloro on his twenty-second birthday.

Now it was one skater, a familiar figure in black T-shirt and black pants, a man famous for his dramatic flair. It was Kurt Browning's turn.

In truth, at that moment in the now-packed Amphitheatre, Kurt didn't face an overwhelming challenge. If he got through his program cleanly, made no mistakes, the chances were solid that the judges would place him among the top three. That seemed a tough chore perhaps, but hardly insurmountable.

And in the first few moments of his routine, it looked as if Kurt was in peak form. He pegged the jump that he had missed two years earlier in Albertville. It was a great start, but from then on, he met disaster at every turn.

It began on the back end of a triple flip. Kurt fell. This was a jump he could perform in his sleep. But simply, inexplicably, he fell.

Things got worse. Kurt needed to do a double Axel in order to complete the necessary elements of the technical program. But he turned the double into a single. In figure skating, the only thing more harmful than falling

on a required element is not trying to perform it at all. Kurt didn't. And in an instant, Kurt Browning had skated himself out of contention for a medal at the 1994 Olympics.

He bowed his head at the end, managed a smile, and skated to the kiss-and-cry area in an amphitheatre that had fallen into a stunned silence. It was eerie, so quiet in the place, so hushed, so shocked.

Then the judges' marks confirmed the horror.

Kurt Browning had placed twelfth.

The man is all class. Other athletes under the same crushing circumstances might have avoided the media. Not Kurt Browning. He wanted to talk about it. When he came to our CTV interview area and sat with us, the sight of his parents nearby, both of them clearly aching over their son's disappointment, brought tears to his eyes. He gathered himself, looked straight into our camera and told Canada that he was sorry. "It's all over," he said. "Maybe it wasn't meant to be."

The funny thing was, he had no reason to apologize. He had already given us so many thrills for so many years that it really didn't matter. You had to wonder about this one though. Kurt Browning deserved better.

Maybe he was right. Maybe, it wasn't meant to be.

DAY SEVEN

Facing page
Myriam Bédard, after
winning her first gold
of the Games

MORNING BRINGS NEW LIGHT

Friday, February 18, 1994.

She made a name for herself in Albertville when she captured a bronze medal and the hearts of Canadians.

Myriam Bédard's story, however, was far from over. In fact, her mission wasn't nearly complete. Albertville, as great as it was for Myriam, was only a warm-up for Lillehammer. But first, a word about her sport, the biathlon.

It's a grueling sport that combines cross-country skiing and rifle shooting. The point is to ski at breakneck speed between targets, pull up at the target areas, and get off the required number of shots. In the 15 km biathlon, which was the event Myriam Bédard was competing in on the morning of Day Seven, there are four different points where each competitor is allowed five shots. The range of difficulty is enormous. After all, the skiing part of the event gets the heart racing, the blood pounding, which is a state not exactly conducive to a steady trigger finger. In the sport, they say the transition from the skiing part to the shooting part is like turning from a rabbit to a stone in a heartbeat.

As a child in Loretteville, Québec, Myriam's first love was figure skating. But the expense of the sport prohibited her from following this interest. As a teenager, Myriam joined the cadets. She learned how to shoot, and then grew into the skiing skills. She had an auspicious start to her sport; at 16, she entered her first competition. Wearing a rented pair of boots with tissue stuffed into the toes, she won.

Myriam says the appeal of the biathlon for her lies in the sport's solitude. She loves hitting the trails alone, by herself, away from noise and commotion, in an isolation that allows her to seek her own destiny.

Individual Biathlon
The first recorded biathlon race was in 1767 by military patrols along the Swedish-Norwegian border. The sport was dropped from the Olympic Games between 1948-56 because of anti-military sentiment, but was reinstated in 1960. In the individual biathlon race there are 4 shooting sessions which alternate between the standing and prone positions. Each shot missed adds a one-minute penalty to the skier's time.

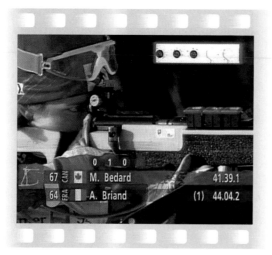

This page and next
Myriam Bédard takes
gold on the 15 km
biathlon course.

Coming into the 1994 Games, Myriam hadn't had a particularly sparkling season. That was by design. She deliberately didn't prime herself for the World Cup events. She was aiming beyond them to the Olympics. And in the five days leading up the 15 km at Lillehammer, she imposed an exile on herself. She took her meals alone, talked to no one, kept her focus on the perfect race, running it over and over in her mind. She was willing herself into a zone.

Perversely, the adoration of the crowd surrounding the 15 km course almost pulled her out of the zone. Myriam was the popular favourite, and her fans let her know how they felt. "What I found hardest," she said after the race, "was everything going on around me. People were yelling, 'Go Myriam, go,' and I was becoming distracted. I had to regain the mental state I'd put myself in over the last five days."

She succeeded in her struggle. Myriam's start position was number 67 out of 70 racers, and, in her super-concentrated state, she absolutely flew through the skiing sections of the race. And she maintained remarkable control on the ranges. She missed a mere two of twenty shots. Her nearest rival, France's Anne Briand, missed three. Going into the final kilometre of the race, Myriam had opened up a forty-second lead. All she had to do was stay in her zone for a few more minutes. She did it, all the way to the finish line, all the way to a gold medal. She had won by more than 46 seconds!

The two other Canadians in the race finished well back. Lise Meloche of Chelsea, Québec was 18th. Calgary's Kristin Berg was 51st.

Later that day, Myriam stood on a stage in downtown Lillehammer. Canadian flags were waving all around her. The Canadian flags hadn't been there in Albertville. She told us

she felt that only her parents had watched her accept the bronze medal then.

Around her neck this time was gold. Her face was glowing. She couldn't stop smiling. *O Canada* played and I was certain at this moment that back in Myriam's hometown of Loretteville, Québec, everyone felt enormous pride for her.

But there was still more work to do. "I will enjoy this tonight," she said, "But tomorrow I will be thinking about the 7.5 km race."

Myriam had Canada's second gold medal of the Games. She would go after another on Wednesday.

Luge is hardly a huge sport in Canada, and at Lillehammer, in the men's doubles luge on the track at Hunderfossen, we were represented by just a single team. It was composed of Bob Casper and Clay Ives. Bob was the veteran of the duo, 35 years old and in his third, and final, Olympics. Clay, at 21 and in his first Games, filled the role of rookie. And these two guys did Canada proud. Rocketing down the chute—on their final run as a team since, after two years together, Bob was retiring—they came in a very respectable eighth against the world's best. They were less than one second behind the gold medal winning time. It was Canada's highest ever finish in Olympic doubles luge.

At the Viking Ship for the men's 5000 m speedskating race, Dan Jansen was the big story. Of course he was. Would Jansen, on his very last crack at an Olympic medal, finally overcome adversity, bad luck, and his opponents and win gold? The question was on everybody's lips.

But for Canadians there were a few others in the race who merited attention.

Luge

This event has been in Olympic competition since 1964, though its origins go back to the Mohawks of Kahnawake in Québec who used "toboggans," an Indian word, to transport goods in the winter. Luge is a timed event. There are no steering or braking mechanisms on the luge sled; the lugers use shifts in their body weight to steer. The course is between 100 and 1500 m in length and its gradient ranges from 8 to 15%. The construction of refrigerated tracks and aerodynamic sleds means that speeds of up to 150km/h are reached.

59

JPN	J. Inoue	(5)	29.8	1.13.75
USA	D. Jansen	(1)	29.1	1.12.43

WR

Kevin Scott of Sault Ste. Marie, Ontario was one. He just happened to be the world record holder in the event, and even if he was competing with a pulled groin muscle, he was a force to be reckoned with.

Then there was Sylvain Bouchard who grew up idolizing Gaétan Boucher, the double gold medalist from the 1984 Olympics. And there were the two Canadian lads with the Irish names, Sean Ireland from Winnipeg and Patrick Kelly of Toronto.

Kelly has the lineage. His dad is Red Kelly, Hockey Hall of Famer, star defenceman for the Detroit Red Wings, star centre for the Toronto Maple Leafs, and Patrick's mom was the former Andra McLaughlin, a figure skater who finished fifth at the 1950 World Championships and then remodelled herself into a North American speedskating champ. Patrick started out following his dad's foot-

steps into hockey, but turned later to speedskating. That's a demanding chore for a man in his twenties. But Patrick made the transition so successfully that he was a member of Canada's team at the Albertville Games. He finished far back in the 1000 m that year, in 45th place, but here he was, at age 31, back for another try in Lillehammer.

As for Dan Jansen, the tension surrounding him before the event was enormous. His family, including wife Robin and baby daughter Jane, sat down near ice level at the oval. Everybody in the building, family or stranger, American or non-American, had the jitters for Dan Jansen.

As he stepped up to the starting line for his run, the place fell into total silence. When the gun sounded the silence was obliterated by the roar of cheers, like a wave following him around the oval with every

stride. The people went wild. They screamed and yelled and hollered for Jansen. And he responded. This time, there would be no slip. This time, there would be no bobble. This time, there would be a straight skate to glory. Jansen barreled around the rink, and when he finished and when his time went up on the board, the numbers read 1:12:43. A new world record! After ten years and seven misses in medal races, Dan Jansen had his gold.

After receiving his medal, Jansen did a victory lap with the Olympic mascots, two Norwegian children. He skated to the sideboards, hugged his wife and picked up his daughter. He then took baby Jane for a skate holding her close to his chest, right next to his gold medal. "Win or lose I was going to go home and live the rest of my life," Jansen later told us. "Now I can do it with a medal."

As for the Canadians, Sylvain Bouchard finished fifth. Patrick Kelly was one place back in sixth. Kevin Scott, even with a pulled groin muscle, managed tenth place, and Sean Ireland came in sixteenth. Not a bad group showing, not at all.

The compulsory portion of the dance competition in figure skating is not ordinarily a big drawing card. Everyone skates the same program, and it is a night that can be monotonous for even the biggest fan. But nothing was ordinary at the Lillehammer dance competition because the king and queen of ice dance were making their return to Olympic competition. These two, Jayne Torvill and Christopher Dean of Great Britain, had revolutionized their sport at the 1984 Sarajevo Games. They danced to the music from *Bolero*, and when they were finished, everybody knew that ice dancing would never be

the same, that Torvill and Dean had broken fresh ground. The Sarajevo judges awarded their grace, beauty and sensuousness with straight 6.0s across the board, and the contest for the gold wasn't even close.

Now, after ten years, after turning professional, the pair were back in the Games and the figure skating world held its breath in anticipation. There were serious questions to be answered. Did Torvill and Dean still have the competitive fire? Or would they, as Kurt Browning, Viktor Petrenko and Brian Boitano had in the men's singles, yield to youth and the years?

"I guess we're really putting it on the line," Dean said before the competition opened, "but this is our life, and we really enjoy the challenge of pushing ourselves. We're in the twilight of our careers, and we want to finish on as high a note as we can."

Jayne Torvill's pre-Olympic mood was similar to her partner's. "It's taking the challenge of something new. We were sort of ready for something new and even though it's kind of old, it's new again. But the fact is that it will be ten years since we last competed in the Olympic Games and we feel that the clock is ticking."

As it turned out, the compulsory section of the dance didn't definitively answer any questions. Torvill and Dean showed plenty of the old magic, but at the end of the day, they stood in third place. Two Russian pairs—Maia Usova and Alexander Zhulin, Oksana Gritschuk and Evgeny Platov—placed ahead of Torvill-Dean. Two more dances were still to come, the original program and the free dance, and it looked as if we had a terrific battle to look forward to.

Canada's team, Shae-Lynn Bourne and Victor Kraatz, would not be in the running,

but they knew that before they came to Norway. The dazzling new dance duo finished 14th at the World Championships in Prague and were making great progress by the day. Their Olympic goal was to crack the top ten and they were on track to do that. They, too, could someday set the dance fraternity on its ear, just like their heroes Torvill and Dean. They have the potential to become the best in the world at this sport.

DAY EIGHT

SILVER SATURDAY

Saturday, February 19, 1994

It doesn't take a visitor long to discover the true passion of the people of Norway. It can be found on the streets, on the trails, in the hills and in the coat of arms of Lillehammer: cross-country skiing. It's like baseball in America. More than just a sport, it's a pasttime, a way of life.

Sure I knew Norwegians liked cross-country skiing. What I didn't know until these Games was that they are fanatics. Consider this: on Day Eight, 100,000 Norwegians turned out in the frigid early morning just to watch the 15 km cross-country men's race. Not only that, some Norwegians, whole families of them in fact, had made camp close to the Birkebeineren cross-country trail in −30° temperatures just to be sure they'd have a choice location to watch the races. This wasn't a camp-out for a night or two. This was for the whole two weeks of the Games.

There's no two ways about it, Norwegians are passionate about cross-country skiing.

And their enthusiasm was rewarded in the 15 km. A Norwegian skier won gold, a familiar Norwegian skier. The winner was the remarkable Bjorn Daehlie who beat out another incredible athlete, Vladimir Smirnov from Kazakhstan. For Smirnov, it was his second medal of the Lillehammer Games. For Daehlie, it was his second gold at these Olympics, the fifth of his career.

Canada's lone cross-country skier at Lillehammer, Dany Bouchard of La Tuque, Québec, called their efforts "super-human." Bouchard finished 52nd.

For Canada, it was a day of mixed results— close to gold in a couple of sports, and we made respectable showings in others.

Going into the women's downhill at Kvitfjell, Canadians had reason for optimism.

This page and next
Susan Auch skates to
silver in the 500m.

Three of our skiers figured to be legitimate contenders for medals, Kate Pace, Michelle Ruthven and Kerrin-Lee Gartner. But the optimism didn't pan out. Germany's Katja Seizinger skied like a woman possessed and put an immediate lock on the gold. Kate Pace made a run that was unspectacular but solid enough to stir thoughts of a possible medal. But in rapid succession, the U.S.'s Picabo Street and Italy's Isolde Kostner blazed faster times than Kate. That meant silver for Street, bronze for Kostner and, ultimately, fifth place for Pace. Gartner and Ruthven, sad to say, were further back with placings of 19th and 30th respectively.

Better news came from the Viking Ship where the women speedskaters were competing in the 500 m event. Nobody expected a gold medal for Canada here, not in a race that Bonnie Blair, the U.S.'s most suc-

cessful female Olympian of all time, practically owned. But Canada had Susan Auch in the race, and Susan had dreams.

Susan grew up in Winnipeg, and it was there, aged twelve, that she took up speed-skating. The way she tells it, she had to make a choice between Brownies and skating. She opted for the skates, and she must have shown immediate promise because two years later, her older sister told Susan that of all the skaters in Winnipeg, it was she, Susan, who would make it to the Olympics one day. Big sister knew best.

Susan turned her sister into a prophet in 1988 when she went to her first Olympics as a member of the short track relay speed-skating team. That team was good enough to take a bronze medal, but after the Games, Susan switched from short track to long track. The new event proved to be a

solid fit for her, and in 1992 she was back in the Olympics at Albertville, competing in the 500 m, racking up a good time of 40.83 and finishing sixth.

At home, Susan took dead aim on the '94 Games. By then, home was in Calgary where she lived a relentless outdoor life, skating in winter, biking and horseback riding in summer, running with her dog, an Australian Blue, through the fields of Nose Hill in Calgary's northwest corner. And all the while, keeping fit, training, working on her technique, Susan set herself for Lillehammer and a medal.

"I think it's possible to have my best possible race at the Olympics," she said before the Games. "I thrive under that kind of pressure. That's when I perform my best."

And so she did. On Day Eight, in the 500 m, Susan exploded off the starting line.

That's her specialty, a burning start, and at the end of the first 100 m, she was .08 of a second ahead of Bonnie Blair. But if a strong start is Susan's strong suit, the rap against her has always been that she's flagged, relatively speaking, over the final 200 metres.

That wasn't the case in this race. Susan hung in, keeping the pace and at the end, Blair beat her by not much more than a blink of an eye. Susan's time was a thrilling 39.61. Blair got the gold, as expected, in 39.25 seconds, her fourth in three Olympics. Susan took silver, the first long track speedskating medal for a Canadian woman in eighteen years.

At the hockey arena, Canada was up against Slovakia, a tough-minded team led by the former NHL star, Peter Stastny. Paul Kariya got the Canadians off to a promising

Facing page
Chris Lori pilots his
sled down the
Hunderfossen run.

This page
Canadians in bob-
sleigh competition.

Bobsleigh

Bobsledding began late in the 1800s when the Swiss attached a mechanism to control the steering of a toboggan. The early sled crews included 2 women crew members with 2 or 3 men but in 1923 it was decided that the sport was too dangerous for women.
To begin the race the crew rocks the sled and then sprints down the track before vaulting into the sled. Speeds of up to 150 km/h are reached and in corners the crew is subjected to G-forces over 6 times their own weight.
The bobsled course is at least 1500 m long with a gradient between 8 and 15%. It must have at least 15 banked curves.
Canada took gold in this event once—1964, with Vic Emery driving his Canadian sled.

start by scoring just over a minute into the game. But the Slovaks tied it up, and the game settled into a routine of hard hitting and determined defensive play. That proved to be to the Slovaks' advantage. They dominated the boards, blocked off the Canadians' usual third-period flurry, and sealed the win with a last-minute empty-net goal that made the score 3–1.

The loss was the bad news for Canada. The good news was that, with their earlier two wins and a tie, Canada's team already had a playoff spot in the bag.

Nothing was in the bag for Canada's bob-sled teams at the Hunderfossen. This was the first of the two days of competition in the two-man event, and Canada had two teams to cheer for.

It takes an enormous amount of skill and courage simply to participate in this sport,

and the teams of Pierre Lueders–Dave MacEachern and Chris Lori–Glenroy Gilbert, weren't lacking in either department. The driver is, of course, the key to success in the two-man event, the one who's responsible for steering the hurtling sled, reaching speeds of up to 150 km/h, through the twists and turns of the icy run. In Lueders and Lori, Canada had two of the best drivers in bobsledding history.

Lori was the veteran of the two, 31-years-old, a driver with a great record in four-man racing as well as in the two-man variety, and the winner of Canada's first ever World Championship in 1990. His style turned on consistency and dependability, and he demonstrated those two qualities at the Albertville Olympics where he steered Canada's four-man sled to fourth place. The heartbreaking part of the Albertville experience was that Lori

and Canada missed out on a bronze medal by just 11/100ths of a second. Lori hoped to erase that raw memory with a medal at the Hunderfossen.

Lueders was, by contrast, the brash rookie. He was 23, Canada's best two-man driver, a young man who thrived on jet-like starts. Like all brash young drivers, he had an occasional tendency to wildness. But who was to question Lueders' style, when he had won the very first World Cup race he entered? He hoped to duplicate that accomplishment in this, his very first Olympics.

But it was not in the cards, not for Lueders, not for Lori. The Lueders–MacEachern team finished the day in seventh place, Lori-Gilbert in fifteenth. Both drivers spoke of disappointment with the ice and in their own performances. Both hoped for better results in the next day's

final runs. But in realistic terms, both had steered themselves out of medal contention.

Out of medal contention. Those were the same words we were using for Kurt Browning. Even as I look at those words on the page, they don't seem right. Kurt Browning not fighting it out for a medal? Kurt Browning not going for gold? Kurt Browning, twelfth after the technical program?

Even in his very first Olympics in Calgary, as a bright-eyed teenager, he finished eighth. But that was 1988, this was 1994. Now as Kurt stepped on the ice for the men's free skate at Northern Lights Hall, we were witnessing a new order in men's figure skating and Kurt, still only 27, belonged to the old.

Kurt skated for pride on this night. He skated for all the people back in Canada who had faxed him their messages of sympathy

and best wishes after his emotional interview on CTV two nights earlier. And he skated for a little redemption, to show everyone that he didn't belong in twelfth place where he'd finished in Thursday's competition.

Maybe Kurt didn't give his greatest performance on this night, but it was very close. He skated the *Casablanca* story; Kurt Browning skated to centre ice and Rick Blaine, his *Casablanca* alter-ego, took it from there. Kurt generated tremendous emotion, and his charm completely captivated the crowd. When he finished, when the music died away, as he stood at the far end of the arena, somehow looking taller and grander, the people in the arena hailed him with applause, cries, flowers and tears. It was a terrific moment. And it was capped off when the judges awarded him marks

that, in the end, moved Kurt all the way up to fifth place in the final standings.

The other members of the old order made similar comebacks. Brian Boitano double-footed his two triple flips, but he landed the triple Axel, and when he did, he gave a broad smile. His performance moved him up to sixth place. Viktor Petrenko skated a better program than he did in his gold medal year at Albertville. He was so good that the Romanian judge awarded him a 6.0 for artistic impression. That helped boost Petrenko to fourth place overall.

So it went through the list of skaters. The U.S.'s Scott Davis ended up eighth. It was ninth for Steven Cousins from Great Britain and an impressive tenth place showing for Sébastien Britten of Brossard, Québec.

But the three skaters everybody was waiting for, the three who would wage the contest

Facing page
Elvis Stojko

This page
Elvis Stojko's free skate,
inspired by music
from The Dragon.

for the gold, were still to come, Canada's Elvis Stojko, France's Philippe Candeloro, and Russia's Alexei Urmanov.

Elvis skated first.

He was up against a couple of obstacles. History was one. No Canadian male skater, not Donald Jackson, not Toller Cranston, not Brian Orser, had won gold at the Olympics. And then, there was the prejudice that Elvis's fans perceived the judges as holding against his rock'n'roll style.

But Elvis looked ready. He looked the way he did on the night he won the Canadian championship, a look compounded of supreme confidence and a hunger to win. He came out to the music from Bruce Lee's biographical film, *The Dragon*, perfect stuff for a young man who holds a black belt in karate. But, right away, unexpectedly, there was a hitch. Elvis pulled out of a triple Axel

and singled. But, thinking on the fly, he compensated by replacing a planned quadruple jump with a triple Axel-triple-toe combination that was perfection. That marked the turning point for Elvis. From then on, he skated a flawless program, and when he finished, everybody in the building knew Elvis had pulled off something special. He looked up into the arena to the spot above the Richmond Hill banner, and when he caught his mom's eye, she gave him the thumbs' up signal. That said it all. In the kiss-and-cry, Doug Leigh, Stojko's coach, embraced choreographer Uschi Keszler, the woman credited with adding the softer touches to the new Elvis.

Then came the marks. For technical merit, seven 5.9s, two 5.8s. That was good. Very good. For artistic impression, 5.8s, 5.7s, a 5.5 from the Russian judge. That

This page and next Elvis's program — powerful, dynamic and technically demanding.

was not good. That was insulting. It appeared that, once again, the judges weren't giving Elvis a break. Still, Elvis was in first place.

Philippe Candeloro, third after the technical program, skated next. He performed to music from *The Godfather*, and he was elegant, attractive, clearly a crowd favourite. He was marked down by missing a triple Axel and hitting the ice near the end of his routine. Still, his marks were high enough to put him in third place at the end of the evening. The bronze medal was his, the first medal won by a French male skater since Patrick Pera's bronze in Sapporo in 1972.

Alexei Urmanov stepped on to the ice, the last skater in the competition, the only man who could take the gold from Elvis Stojko. To watch Urmanov's performance, Elvis climbed into the stands and sat with Kurt Browning, right beside our ice-level broad-

cast position. It must have been tough on Elvis, waiting, watching, knowing that your own ultimate fate depends not on yourself but on what someone else accomplishes.

Urmanov skated, as usual, exquisitely. He completed an impressive eight triples. But his routine wasn't without flaws. On a triple flip, he tripped on the landing, almost hit the boards, and just managed to stay on his feet. Who could predict what the judges would make of that?

We didn't have to wait long to find out.

Urmanov's marks came up. For technical merit, 5.8s and 5.7s. It looked good for Elvis.

For artistic impression, 5.7s, 5.8s, 5.9s. Now it looked good for Urmanov. Very, very good. He got the gold medal. Elvis had to settle for silver.

Brian Orser, in our broadcast area, talking live to Canada, happened to glance up. Elvis

was looking at him. Elvis winked. Brian nodded back. These two had much in common, both of them charter members of the Canadian male skaters' silver medal club.

Many in the crowd, especially the Canadian contingent, felt that the judges had robbed Elvis. Elvis himself offered no signs of protest, but when he spoke to us later, he showed some disappointment.

"As soon as I started the program, right through to the end, I skated free," he said. "Nothing can take that away from me, no matter what a judge says or people think. It's a matter of opinion. It's the best skate I've ever had under such circumstances. I challenged myself and I won."

That was Elvis, a leader in the new wave of great men figure skaters.

DAY NINE

Facing page
Another Norwegian
fan turning out to
hail "Koss the Boss."

HAIL THE KING

Sunday, February 20, 1994

The Norwegian crowds began to arrive at the Viking Ship in Hamar very early and in large numbers on the morning of Day Nine. This was a festive bunch, people with painted faces, wearing horned Viking helmets, waving Norwegian flags. They had come to pay tribute to the man who was hailed in a sign that one fan carried: "Koss is Boss." Koss was, of course, the mighty Johann Olav Koss, the Norwegian speedskater who had already won gold medals and set world records in these Games in the 1500 m and the 5000 m. Now he was going for a third gold in the longest, most grinding distance of all, the 10 000 m.

In the middle of the oval at the Viking Ship, serving as an inspiration and example to Koss, stood a statue of a great Norwegian speedskater from a past era. His name was Hjalmar "Hjallis" Andersen, and 42 years earlier, at the Oslo Games of 1952, he had

accomplished exactly the feat that Koss was setting out to complete on this day. Andersen won gold in all three races, 1500 m, 5000 m and 10 000 m. The statue of Andersen, still a great hero in Norway, shows him, fittingly, with his hands in the air in victory, frozen in time and triumph.

Someone suggested to Koss, after his second gold medal, that one day a similar statue of him, of Koss, might be erected to celebrate his victories. Koss laughed. Much better, he said, to spend the money on Olympic Aid for the suffering people of Sarajevo.

If any of Koss's fans in the Viking Ship entertained the slightest worry that he could miss on a third gold, Koss took care of the concern in record time. "Record time" were the operative words. He flashed around the oval, all 10 000 metres, faster than any man in history. He blew away the

Ski Jumping
The first ski jumping competition was held in Norway in 1862 and it has been an Olympic event since 1924 at Chamonix, France. Scores are given by judges who award points for the length of the jump, style, form and landing. Length accounts for 50% of the total score. The K-point (critical point) is marked by a line in the snow and marks are deducted for every metre a skier falls short of this point. Points are awarded for every metre attained beyond the K-point.

previous record by 12.99 seconds. His closest competitor in the race, Norwegian Kjell Storelid, was so far back he was practically out of sight. Koss beat him by nineteen seconds. It was an astounding athletic performance, one that the bronze medalist, Bart Veldcamp of the Netherlands, predicted would "stand for thirty years."

Koss, the triple gold medalist, was, typically, much more modest. "I could not imagine it was possible to skate like that," he said afterwards. "I am maybe in shock."

Norway was hoping that another of its native sons, Espen Bredesen, would give them the same kind of success in ski jumping. This was a sport that Norwegians had once dominated, but in recent years, they'd been eclipsed by the Finns, the Austrians and the Japanese. The hope was that Bredesen would restore lost glory to Norway.

Two years earlier, after the 1992 Games, nobody would have counted on Bredesen for much. After all, at Albertville, in two competitions, he had finished dead last and third from last. Some people were sarcastically calling him "Espen the Eagle," a not-so-subtle reference to "Eddie the Eagle" Edwards, the British jumper who barely made it down the hill in Calgary.

But the not-quite-young man from Oslo—Bredesen was 26—applied himself to his sport with formidable dedication. He had won two World Championships, and going into the Lillehammer Games, he pronounced himself in the best physical shape of his life.

What Bredesen hadn't foreseen, what his Norwegian fans couldn't have predicted, was the resurrection of Jens Weissflog. Weissflog, a German, had blazed into Olympic consciousness a full ten years earlier when he

*This page and previous
Espen Bredesen of
Norway wins silver in
ski jumping.*

took the ski jumping gold at Sarajevo. He was only nineteen years old at the time, and no one expected him to still be jumping a whole decade later. But he showed up at Lillehammer, and he showed the field the back of his skis. He won gold and left the silver for Espen Bredesen who accepted the setback with superb sportsmanship.

"I didn't lose the gold," Bredesen said. "I won the silver."

As for Canada, we had no entrant in the ski jumping event, and that was a situation that angered Horst Bulau. Horst was the man who achieved Canada's best-ever ski jump result at the Olympics, a seventh in the K120 event at Calgary in 1988. Now, at Lillehammer, Horst was serving as a CTV commentator, and his point was that Canada's best jumper, John Lockyer deserved a chance to compete. The Canadian champion didn't meet qualifying standards before the Games; he was watching this event on television back home in Thunder Bay, Ontario. Lockyer would have benefitted from the experience, would have learned much about his sport, would have received a competitive shot in the soul. Canada, Horst said, needed to pump the same effort into its ski jumping program as it had into its rowing program. Look at the rowers in Barcelona, four golds and a bronze. The same thing could be repeated in ski jumping. Even the silver medallist here, Espen Bredesen, had gone from dead last at Albertville to the silver medal. There was no better example of what experience could do. Horst had a point.

Meanwhile, at Hunderfossen, in the second day of the two-man bobsled competition, neither Canadian sled could make up for time lost in their first runs. Pierre

Eddie the Eagle
Michael "Eddie the Eagle" Edwards was one of the most famous last place finishers of all time. Edwards, a plasterer by trade, worked on his aerodynamics for ski jumping at Calgary's Olympics by strapping himself to the roof rack of his truck and driving the back roads of England. He might as well have used the vehicle in the actual competition where he finished with less than half the points of his nearest rival.

Lueders and Dave MacEachern finished overall in seventh place, and it was fifteenth for Chris Lori and Glenroy Gilbert. That spoiled a potentially unique double that Gilbert was going for. In the summers, he's a premier sprinter, a member of Canada's 4 x 100 m relay team which took bronze at the World Championships. He was hoping to win medals at both the Summer and Winter Olympics, but those hopes were dashed, at least temporarily.

So, by the way, were the dreams of the unlikely bobsled duo from Jamaica, Dudley Stokes and Wayne Thomas. They were disqualified when they weighed in eight pounds over the limit.

The gold medal winners in the two-man were the Swiss team of Gustav Weder and Donat Acklin who repeated their gold medal triumph of the Albertville Games.

At the Northern Lights Hall it was time for romance. The ice dancers were back to do their original dances, these graceful couples who exude sensuality on skates, holding hands, holding eye contact, holding one another close, holding the audience in the spell of the romance they portray.

The Canadian couple, Shae-Lynn Bourne and Victor Kraatz, represented the epitome of romance. Even their first meeting was tinged with a kind of romantic aura. It was in 1992, and Victor's original partner had been forced out of the sport with an injury. Victor and his coach in Montréal, Josée Picard, were searching desperately for a replacement. Victor was on the edge of quitting and taking a job back home in Vancouver when Shae-Lynn came along. The odds seemed long that Shae-Lynn would fit in since she was a pairs skater on the hunt for a new partner of her own. But

Victor and Shae-Lynn stepped onto the ice, and, instantly, within two glides and a touch of the hands, Victor felt captivated.

"I can't describe Shae-Lynn in just a few words," he says. "I would say she's very mysterious. She tells you what she thinks but only if you ask. She's very caring, very passionate about the things she does. She knows what she's doing. We became friends right away."

Their idols in the dance world were, of course, Jayne Torvill and Christopher Dean, and now, at the Lillehammer Games, Shae-Lynn and Victor were sharing the ice and the competition with the two legends of the sport. In a way, it was enough just to skate out a dream, the dream of actually performing in the Olympics. So they went out on the ice, skated beautifully, and at the end of the night, with the free dance still to come on the following evening, they were in the position they had modestly aimed for, tenth place.

Torvill and Dean were in first place. They skated to a rumba, and they filled the building with their familiar magic. The performance moved them up to top spot, but with the two Russian pairs—Usova and Zhulin, Gritschuk and Platov—looking in wonderful form too, it was still a wide-open contest for the gold.

DAY TEN

ON BOARDS AND BLADES

Monday, February 21, 1994

The morning sun was barely peeking over the hilltops and already downtown Lillehammer was wide awake. By now we were almost used to all the frantic activity of the *storgata*. This was the name of the part of Lillehammer's main street that attracted the Olympic crowds. They came to buy souvenirs, to trade pins, to scout for a meal. The area attracted everyone— tourists, locals, athletes, the media—all manner of people squeezing into a space only about ten metres wide by a couple of kilometres long. It was the place to see and be seen, to meet new friends and reunite with old buddies. Everybody made it to the *storgata*, even David Letterman's mom. She was spotted there late one night for two purposes. First, she filed a report to her son's TV show back in New York. Then, like everybody else, she shopped.

On the morning of Day Ten, the Norwegians weren't lingering on the *storgata*. They were passing through, on their way to a number of venues to take in all the sporting activity. We were developing a tremendous respect for the Norwegians as sports fans. They packed the buildings, lined the runs, stood in the cold for each and every sport. They ignored nothing and, in most cases, they made attendance at events a family activity. Schools had been closed for the duration of the Games, and most sports turned into an occasion for mom, dad and the kids to share the Olympic experience together.

The first stop for many of them on Day Ten was the Birkebeineren Stadium for the women's 4 x 5 km cross-country relay. The Norwegians entered a solid team in the race, and it came away with the silver medal. It was the Russians who grabbed the

Unique souvenir
Olympic souvenir sales were, as one would imagine, very brisk. All items with the five interlocking Olympic rings-shirts, hats, flags, trolls, spoons, knives-were in big demand. But the most unusual souvenir was a piece of jewelry: moose dropping earrings. Actual clumps of the material were affixed to silver: the price tag-only $25.

85

gold, a Russian team that was anchored by the inimitable Lyubov Egorova. This was her third gold medal of these Games, the sixth gold in her overall career, a record that tied her with the Soviet speedskating star, Lydia Skoblikova. For Egorova, the medal became number nine in her collection of Olympic medals, just one shy of the ten career medals won by the Russian cross-country legend, Raisa Smetanina.

To most of us Canadians, the real star over at the Kanthaugen Freestyle Arena, where a mogul run was transformed into a launching pad for aerial eliminations, wasn't a competitor. The real star was a coach, a "special coach" of Canada's national team as he was officially called, and he was "special" in more ways than anyone could count.

His name was Yves LaRoche, and he had been one of the original flyers of freestyle skiing, a charter member of the Québec Air Force. Later he coached the national team. Later still, he suffered a tragic paragliding accident that left him in a state of paralysis. Recovery seemed completely out of the question, but over the years LaRoche applied to his broken body the same regimen of courage and toughness that he had brought to his sport. And gradually, his motor skills began to come back. First, he regained partial use of his muscles. Then his speech returned. Then, almost miraculously, Yves LaRoche stood up and walked.

Maybe he wasn't nimble on his feet, maybe he wasn't articulate in his speech, but he'd come back far enough to involve himself once again in the sport he loved. He turned up at the Lac Beaumont water course in Québec where aerialists practice in the off-season and offered his wisdom and expertise to the young people who aspired to emulate Yves.

One of them was the younger LaRoche, Yves' brother, Philippe, who was by then the World Champion. Philippe listened to Yves, and so did all the others.

They were still listening to their "special coach" at the Kanthaugen Freestyle Arena and at the end of the day, the team of Philippe LaRoche, Lloyd Langlois, Nicolas Fontaine and Andy Capicik—the Air Force, the best team in the world—had qualified for the men's final. And just for good measure, Canada's Caroline Olivier qualified for the women's final. They did Yves LaRoche proud.

There was action of every sort on Day Ten.

At the Viking Ship, the great American speedskater, Bonnie Blair, missed a fifth career medal by .03 seconds. The event was the 1500 m, and Blair came in fourth, just the tiniest margin behind the bronze medalist, Gunda Niemann of Germany. The gold went to Austria's Emese Hunyady. Saskatoon's Catriona Le May made the best showing for Canada in seventeenth place.

The Canadians looked sharper in hockey beating the strong Swedish squad by a single goal, 3–2, with Chris Kontos, Todd Hlushko and Petr Nedved handling the scoring. The game ended the round robin section of the hockey competition, and sent Canada into a quarter-final match against the Czechs. The match-ups were set. In two days the medal round would begin.

In the evening, it was back to the Northern Lights Hall for another round of romance—the free dance competition among Torvill–Dean and the two Russian couples.

But first, before the medal contenders took to the ice, it was time for the two young Canadians to play out their dream. Shae-Lynn Bourne and Victor Kraatz performed a

This page and next
Grichtchuk and
Platov, of Russia, take
the gold in the ice
dance competition.

Oksana Grichtchuk
& Yevgeny Platov

Russian gypsy routine that packed drama and elegance. They seemed almost to float, and when they finished and sat in the kiss-and-cry area, they looked as if they didn't want ever to get up and leave.

"This was beyond our wildest dreams," Victor told us later. "We can't wait to get back here again.

Victor and Shae-Lynn had gone into the competition aiming for tenth place, and at the end of the judging, they got what they wanted.

This was more than could be said for Jayne Torvill and Christopher Dean. There was nothing wrong with their performance on this night. In fact, doing their Fred and Ginger, making the ice surface seem like a polished ballroom dance floor, they were terrific, and the audience gave them a standing ovation. The trouble came when the judges' marks were

announced. That's when the audience broke into boos. That's when Torvill and Dean—Dean looking peeved in the kiss-and-cry area, Torvill managing a game smile—knew they wouldn't win gold, that they'd have to settle for bronze.

There might have been an explanation for the Torvill–Dean fall from the peak. Earlier in the season, after the couple had won narrowly at the European Championships, Dean had pronounced himself unhappy with their free skate. He said it needed an overhaul, and since Dean is a man of his convictions, he reworked eighty percent of the free skate routine in the weeks before the Games. It may have been that, with all the rearranged material, Torvill and Dean sacrificed some of their acclaimed smoothness. That was an explanation but not an excuse.

With the favourites out of the picture, the two Russian couples danced for the

gold. Maia Usova and Alexander Zhulin might have been the choice on form since they held the 1993 world dance championship. But it was Oksana Gritschuk and Evgeny Platov who prevailed. And they did it with an unRussian-like rock'n'roll routine that had the arena hopping and bopping. They rocked all the way to the gold.

At the medal ceremony, however, it wasn't this deserving couple who rated the loudest cheers from the audience. The noise was saved for the bronze medalists, Torvill and Dean. Maybe that was just sentiment, maybe it was a kind of farewell tribute, or maybe it was yet another reflection of the subjectivity in this most subjective of sports. Indeed, the controversy over Torvill–Dean's third place finish continued for days after. The International Skating Union defended the judging at the Olympic dance competition, arguing that the

couple had been correctly penalized for illegal moves. According to the ISU, Torvill–Dean finished exactly where they belonged. And the controversy raged on.

Driving back to Lillehammer from Hamar this night after the skate dance competition, we noticed the skies above us begin to lighten. We stopped the car, got out and looked up at heavens that were streaking with brilliant light. It was the *aurora borealis*, the northern lights. All of us had seen this beautiful phenomenon back home in Canada. All of us had seen it portrayed on the official emblem of the Lillehammer Games. But none of us had seen it in such pure, glorious green and gold, shimmering across the sky, dancing over the valley, as we did on this magical night.

The Norwegians sure know how to put on a show!

DAY ELEVEN

FULL MOON FEVER

Tuesday, February 22, 1994

Every television producer who covers the Olympics draws a big black circle around the second Tuesday of the Games. That's invariably the lightest day on the schedule, the day when fewest events take place, and it's also the time when most broadcast crews begin to feel the grind. The idea is if we can survive the day and come out of it with renewed spirits, there'll be clear sailing to the end of the Games.

Black Tuesday at Lillehammer began with another stunning sunrise, a pot of strong coffee, and the prospect for a soft slate of activities. Soft? Well, soft except for the evening's events at the Northern Lights Hall over in Hamar. That's when we'd cover the action in short track speedskating. This was a comparatively new sport to the Olympics. The short track people had participated at Albertville for the first time as a fully recognized sport after a tryout year in Calgary where it was consigned the status of demonstration sport. Now it was entirely accepted. Now people realized it was a wild and crazy sport, sort of mayhem on skates. And now people knew that Canada was a power in the game.

But first on Day Eleven, the usual 100,000 spectators trekked out to the Birkebeineren cross-country stadium for the men's 4 x 10 km relay. Norway, with a team propped up by the heroic Bjorn Daehlie, looked like the favourite. But it was the Italian team who took the gold medal when its relay anchor, Silvio Fauner, nipped Daehlie by 0.4 seconds. That was Daehlie's second silver to go with his two golds. But the man who was happiest on this day was Italy's second skier, leader and inspiration, Maurilio De Zolt. For him, it was vindication at last, a gold medal at last, a magnificent achievement for a man who was 43 years old.

The Fijian Team
The smallest national team in Lillehammer was from Fiji. There was one member. He was cross-country skier Rusiate Rogoyawa who finished 88th, dead last, in the 10 km classic race. Rusiate took up the sport as an exchange student and in these Games he finished 14 minutes behind the gold medalist, Bjorn Daehlie. The Norwegian fans gave him a huge ovation. "He is a great sportsman like Daehlie," said one spectator. "Daehlie wins. Rogoyawa tries... it is as important."

91

This page and next Canada's women short track speed-skaters, a medal possibility slips away.

Short Track Speedskating

Short track speedskaters race counter-clockwise around a 111 m oval track. Their high speeds combined with the sharp turns of the track make this sport a dangerous one.

Most speedskaters skate in both the individual races and the relays. Elimination rounds precede the final; skaters are only allowed a 20-minute rest between races and all rounds, including the final, are skated in one day. Short track speedskating began in the early 1900s. The first world championships were in 1978 and this event debuted at the Calgary Games as a demonstration sport. In Albertville, it attained full medal status.

"He's almost old enough to be my father," Daehlie said of De Zolt later. "I doubt I'll be able to ski that fast when I'm 43."

Next the huge crowds moved on to Lysgaardsbakkene for the team K120 ski jump. This came down to a fight for the gold between Germany and Japan. The Germans were led by the red-hot large-hill individual champion, Jens Weissflog, but Japan had the gold practically in its grasp until Masahiko Harada came up short on his last jump. He came *way* short, almost 40 metres behind Weissflog's final leap. Harada was so distraught over costing his country the gold that he sank to his knees in the snow, sobbing.

Sunset over Hamar brought a full moon over Northern Lights Hall. It was the perfect setting for the crazy ride that short track speedskating would take us on.

There certainly had been a personality change in the building from the previous night when dance was the theme and the audience suitably reserved. Forget the soft touches of the tango; this was loud, in-your-face, mayhem. Just the way short trackers like it.

The Koreans were among the loudest in the building. Waving banners, blowing horns, yelling Korean cheers.

The Koreans' biggest challenge would be the Canadian team.

Canada, a power in short track speedskating? It sounds odd, but it's entirely true. Actually the statement needs some adjusting. It's not all of Canada that drives our short track success. It's Québec.

It's Québec that boasts the many clubs where short track speedskating is a teaching priority. And it's Québec where the great skater Gaétan Boucher is held with such awe

and respect. True enough, Boucher was a long track skater, but when it comes to matters of ice and speed, young kids don't draw much of a difference between long track and short track. They're simply looking for speed, and Gaétan Boucher is their prime model.

So it's been no accident that Canada, specifically Québec, has produced such stars of short track speedskating as Nathalie Lambert, the reigning women's world champion at the time of the Lillehammer Games. There's also Marc Gagnon, Nathalie's male counterpart, only nineteen but the men's world champ.

The women's 3000 m relay team looked particularly strong for Canada at Lillehammer. The Canadian skaters had won the gold in this event in the 1992 Albertville Olympics, and even though the team had undergone a couple of adjustments, the lineup of Nathalie

Lambert, Isabelle Charest, Christine Boudrias and Sylvie Daigle seemed golden.

Daigle's story was the most intriguing. She hadn't planned to skate at these Olympics. She was supposed to be in retirement, studying medicine back home in Canada, content with having skated on the 3000 m gold medal-winning team of 1992. But something rankled Sylvie from the Albertville Games. In the semi-finals of the 500 m singles her skates had clashed with those of the U.S.'s Cathy Turner. The collision fractured one of Sylvie's blades, and she was out of the race. This wasn't supposed to happen, not to Sylvie Daigle, a five-time World Champion, a three-time Olympian. And later, even in retirement, the memory of that disaster pulled her back to the 1994 Olympics.

"I feel like there's unfinished business," she told us. "I prepared myself for Albertville

Gaétan Boucher
Gaétan Boucher was born May 10, 1958 at Charlesbourg, Québec. In the long track speedskating events at the 1984 Olympics in Sarajevo he took gold medals in the 1000 m and 1500 m events and a bronze in the 500 m race. He also won a silver medal in 1980 in the 1000 m at Lake Placid, placing second to the great Eric Heiden. Gaétan has been an inspiration to a generation of Quebeckers in speedskating. His legacy can be seen in the strength of the Canadian teams, both men and women, at Lillehammer.

Eric Heiden

At 17, speedskater Eric
Heiden competed in
Innsbruck's Games
and came away empty-
handed. Four years
later, playing to the
home crowd in Lake
Placid, the American
became the first and
only athlete to win five
gold medals in one
Games. He retired, a
21-year-old Olympic
legend, at the end of
that 1980 season.

and I wanted to be satisfied with my performance. So I was really disappointed, frustrat-
ed and sad. I didn't accomplish what I set out
to do."

The Canadian women opened strongly
enough in the 3000 m relay against the
Americans, Chinese and South Koreans. All
four women—Lambert, Charest, Boudrias and
Daigle—were putting away the laps, pushing
off, one to the other, and looking powerful.

Still, the very nature of short track skating
invites catastrophe. This is a sport in which
the skaters fly around the track, hunched
over, fingers touching the ice for balance—a
sport that mixes strength and finesse to the
ultimate degree. Then there's the complicat-
ing factor of the competitors trying to claim
their share of the racing ice. Contact between
rivals is absolutely prohibited in short track
skating, and when a referee determines that

one skater bumped another or that one skater
even took another's line, then the offender can
be disqualified. So, not only is the sport fast
and intricate, it's rigidly policed. Or, at least
it's supposed to be.

Trouble for Canada came when Christine
Boudrias negotiated a bad turn and flew off
into a corner up against the boards. She had
managed to tag off, but, realistically, Canada
was out of the race for the gold.

The Canadians skated hard in the fight
over third place, and then they grabbed a
piece of good fortune. An American skater
fell. Canada moved up to third, and that's
where they remained at the finish line. It
was gold for South Korea, silver for China,
bronze for Canada.

But hold on!

Just as the women were falling into line for
the march on to the ice to receive their gold,

silver and bronze medals, the judges stepped in. They announced that the Chinese had been disqualified for interference. It was a late call, but it stuck. And it meant that Canada moved up to silver. Christine Boudrias could feel slightly less stricken over her fall.

Christine, still with tears in her eyes on the podium, perked up. But the happiest of all the competitors was Kim Yoon Mi of South Korea. She had won a gold, and she had also broken a record set at the 1928 Games by the fabled Norwegian figure skater, Sonja Henie. Henie won gold that year, fifteen years old, the youngest competitor ever to take an Olympic gold medal. Kim Yoon Mi, a member of the gold South Korean short track speedskating relay team, was all of thirteen.

If the women's 3000 m relay produced bizarre results for Canada, that was nothing compared to what went on in the men's 1000 m singles. Two Canadians skated through to the semi-finals, Marc Gagnon in one and Derrick Campbell in the other, and at this point full moon mania set in.

First up, Marc Gagnon. As the world champion, he knew the ropes, knew the cat-and-mouse game he had to play in order to finish among the top two and move to the finals. He stuck to script until the split second when he stumbled on a tiny lane marker and fell. That stumble put him out of the race, out of medal contention and into the B-final.

Or so we all thought.

Then came Derrick Campbell. No problem. He skated well in his semi-final, finished second and moved to the finals against Nicholas Gooch of Great Britain and two South Koreans, Ji-Hoon Chae and the favourite, Ki-Hoon Kim. In the finals, Derrick skated with strength and care, seeking to avoid

the calamity that had claimed Marc Gagnon. But no amount of caution could prevent a collision between Derrick and Britain's Gooch. Derrick Campbell crashed into the padded sideboards. Gooch was the skater who would eventually be disqualified. Derrick chased after the two South Koreans in relentless but hopeless pursuit, and ended in third place. A bronze medal for Derrick and for Canada.

Or so we thought.

The judges announced the Derrick had not finished the race, that he had skated off the ice before he reached the finishing line. He was disqualified.

Derrick looked like a thunderbolt had struck him.

"I was certain I completed the race," he told us later. "I heard a bell sound. I thought that meant I was finished. I just can't believe this happened."

With Derrick out of the picture, with Nicholas Gooch of Great Britain disqualified, the bronze medal would go to the winner of the B-final. He was none other than Marc Gagnon.

Marc smiled during the medal ceremony, but he looked uncomfortable. And afterwards, he tried to press the bronze medal on Derrick Campbell.

"Don't worry," Derrick said, refusing the offer, "we'll get one back in the relay."

In short track speedskating, anything was possible.

It was still a historic day for Canada. The two short track medals brought the Olympic team's total at these Games to eight, surpassing the old record of seven, set both in 1932 and 1992. More medals than ever before and there were still five days of competition to go.

DAY TWELVE

Facing page
*Myriam Bédard
proudly displays her
two gold medals.*

MYRIAM'S MESSAGE

Wednesday, February 23, 1994

Myriam Bédard wasn't finished.

She had already won the 15 km biathlon at these Games. She had already captivated Canada. She had already turned her hometown, Loretteville, Québec, into one massive block party of celebration. And she had already sent Lillehammer's fax machines and telephones into overdrive with messages of pride and congratulations from friends, compatriots and total strangers.

Now she was getting set to do everything all over again in the 7.5 km. But this race had a different atmosphere than the 15 km, a different drama, a different set of circumstances.

For one thing, Myriam went into the race with a slightly adjusted mindset. "I don't want to say I wasn't as ready as I was for the last race," she explained. "I was prepared, but I really just wanted to come and have fun."

For another thing, unknown to Myriam, she was competing with one strike against her. All cross-country skiers know that proper waxing of the skis is of paramount importance to glide and thus, speed. What Myriam didn't know until after the race, was that she was operating on mismatched skis, one waxed for cold snow, the other for warmer conditions.

It was a good thing her competitors didn't know.

Svetlana Paramygina of Belarus pushed Myriam the hardest, finishing a scant second behind the Canadian's time. But probably the severest challenge, certainly the most dramatic, came from Inna Sheshilki of Kazakhstan. When Sheshilki entered the stadium at the end of her run, Myriam had finished. She could only stand and watch as Sheshilki made her drive to catch Myriam and seize the gold.

She seemed to have plenty of power down the back stretch, this remarkable young woman, but just as she drew close to the end, a matter of metres from the finish line, her body closed down. She was out of fuel and, spent, exhausted, she slumped to the snow. The milli-seconds ticked past. Sheshilki moved only fractionally. But she wasn't a quitter. She drew on her last reserves of energy and lunged across the finish line. The collapse had cost her a medal. The gallant Sheshilki finished in fourth place.

It was gold for Myriam Bédard, and among Canadians that put her in an elite group. Only one other athlete from Canada had ever won two gold medals at a single Winter Olympics, and he was at Lillehammer. He was working with the French-language TVA network, and he was delighted for Myriam. Gaétan Boucher knew someone would match his record some day.

One group of guys drew special inspiration from Myriam's performance at the Lillehammer Olympics. This was Canada's hockey team, waiting on Day Twelve to meet the Czechs in a quarter-final match. Less than 24 hours earlier, Myriam had been their guest at a team dinner, and she had pumped them up with a serious game of show-and-tell.

"She showed the guys the gold medal she won in the 15 km, and their eyes lit up," hockey coach Tom Renney told us. "She talked about mental toughness. She told them if they wanted a dream bad enough, they could reach for it. That really hit home."

The players needed every edge they could find. One loss would end their Olympics. One loss would dissolve their medal dreams. If they beat Czechoslovakia, they'd move to the semi-finals against the winner of the Finn—U.S. game. In the other bracket, the

matches pitted Slovakia against Russia, Germany against Sweden. Only the best teams were left in contention, and the unheralded Canadians could be excused for an attack of nerves.

No one had more reason to be apprehensive than Petr Nedved. He was in the unsettling position of playing for his new country against his old homeland. He'd defected from Czechoslovakia when he was still a teenage hockey sensation. Then he played his way into the NHL. Then he'd fallen into a contract dispute with the Vancouver Canucks. By such a circuitous route, he found himself in Lillehammer wearing what he affectionately called "the Red Leaf," and yearning with a passion to show his former countrymen what a splendid hockey player he'd become.

In the first period of play, some of the Canadian pre-game nerves seemed to be still on display. It wasn't for lack of support in the Ice Cavern; the arena seats 5500 people, and it looked as if about 3000 of them were waving Canadian flags. But the Czechs dominated Canada through the early play, and with less than a minute left in the first period, they scored when Otakar Janecky intercepted a Greg Johnson pass and beat Corey Hirsch.

Canada got that one back in the second on a sparkling effort by Brian Savage, but late in the period, a goal by Jiri Kucera sent Czechoslovakia back in front. Again it was Brian Savage who evened things up, this time off a terrific pass from Dwayne Norris, delivered one-handed with a Czech player in the process of hauling him down. Tie game, 2–2, and play went into overtime. If no one scored after ten minutes of extra play, then we'd go to a shootout.

It wouldn't get that far.

Canada got a break at the five-minute mark of overtime when the referee whistled a penalty against Czechoslovakia. The face-off was to the left of Czech goalie Petr Briza. Who took the face-off for Canada? Petr Nedved. Who won the draw? Nedved. He slid the puck back to Chris Kontos who swept it to defenceman Brad Werenka. Werenka shot. Someone blocked the puck in front of the net, and it bounced on to Paul Kariya's stick. Kariya fired. He scored.

"It's the biggest goal I've scored in my life," Kariya told us afterwards. "Now we're one win away from playing for the gold."

Brian Savage, one day before he would turn 23, couldn't have asked for a better birthday gift. "This is what we've been working for," the Sudbury goalscorer said. "No one believed in us before this tournament began. But we believed and now look where we are. This is great."

Petr Nedved thanked Myriam Bédard. "I don't know if it was looking at the gold medal or what, but I really believed the things she told us last night helped pull us through. I mean we were behind most of the game. When we needed to show what kind of a team we are, we did."

But the next game, the semi-final match, would be even more demanding than the Czech game. Canada would meet Finland who crushed the Americans in their quarter-final, 6–1. Sweden and Russia came out the winners in the other bracket. Russia's victory was as thrilling as Canada's, 3–2 in overtime against Slovakia. That was the win that drew a most uncharacteristic reaction from the usually dour Russian coach, Victor Tikhonov, long-time veteran of international hockey wars. Tikhonov, caught by the cameras, looked like something between a jumping jack

and a kangaroo. He hopped behind the Russian bench, hugging his assistants, pumping his arm in the air, wearing a grin that threatened to split his face. It was priceless stuff, almost as priceless as Canada's overtime win.

It was a day of big names and big finishes at the Games. In the men's giant slalom, Germany's Markus Wasmeier beat Urs Kaelin of Switzerland by 0.02 seconds, the slimmest margin in Olympic alpine history. And Bonnie Blair, the gracious 29-year-old American, wound up her Olympic career by blowing away the field in the 1000 m race, skating her second best-ever time in the process, winning her second gold of the Games, and her fifth gold overall, more than any other American woman in Olympic history. It was that kind of day, a history-making day, but in pure public relations terms, in hype

and media fascination, it was a day when one event put everything else at the Games in the shade. This was the day when Nancy met Tonya on the ice.

Outside the Northern Lights Hall in Hamar, scalpers were asking and getting $2000 per ticket for the women's figure skating technical program. That was ten times the ticket's face value, and although there were skaters of immense talent in the competition—Katarina Witt back from the pros, 1993 World and European champion Oksana Baiul of the Ukraine, the athletic Surya Bonaly from France—it was undoubtedly the Nancy and Tonya Show that was drawing the most interest.

Since their arrival in Lillehammer, those two seemed to have withstood the media onslaught with poise and control. Harding denied any personal connection to the assault

on Kerrigan. She said there was just one thing on her mind, the gold medal. Kerrigan took the same line. In practice sessions, she showed few after-effects from the assault, and she said, yes, she too was just happy to be in Lillehammer, happy to go for gold.

In an almost perverse way, it may have been the other skaters, not Harding and Kerrigan, who suffered more from the Harding-Kerrigan fallout. Perhaps that was the case with Canada's Susan Humphreys. She wouldn't have dreamed of citing the media distraction as an excuse for what turned out to be a disappointing performance on this night. But Susan was, after all, just eighteen, competing in her first Olympics. She was still fresh from what was, in effect, her coming-out party—her second place finish at the Canadian Championships a month earlier in her home town, Edmonton.

Add up all of those factors, and toss in the bad luck to draw the first skating position in the evening's competition, and it's small wonder that Susan didn't show her finest stuff. She fell on a double-lutz, and the judges marked her so low that she would eventually finish 26th out of 27 and not be permitted to skate in Friday's long program. Susan missed the cut.

If Canadian eyes watered for Susan, Canadian tears flowed for Josée Chouinard. Going into the Games, Josée figured to be a medal contender. She was the Canadian champion, she had plenty of experience, she radiated charm and warmth on the ice. The knock on Josée was that the spark she showed skating in front of Canadian crowds vanished in international competition. To steel herself against that possibility in Lillehammer, she had moved from Montreal

Barbara Ann Scott
In Davos, Switzerland, in 1948, Barbara Ann skated onto an outdoor ice surface that was badly chewed up from two hockey games. She negotiated her way flawlessly around the holes and ruts to become a 19-year-old figure skating queen. She brought Olympic gold home to Canada and became a hero. The name of choice for baby girls that year was Barbara.

This page and next Oksana Baiul skates to second place in the technical program.

to Toronto where she worked at the Granite Club under coach Louis Stong and choreographer Sandra Bezic. The move also put her on the same practice ice as Kurt Browning. If Josée's meticulous preparations worked, then she hoped her past international experiences—ninth at Albertville, ninth at the 1993 World Championships in Prague—would fade away like a bad dream.

Instead the nightmare continued. In her technical program, Josée fell on her triple-Lutz. She didn't complete her double-toe combination. The mistakes were costing her major marks, and when the music ended, as Josée skated off the ice, she wore an expression that reminded me of the one on Kurt Browning's face a few nights earlier. Josée looked devastated. After the night was over, she would stand in eighth place, once again out of medal contention in an international event, the biggest international event of them all.

Among the other skaters, the big names and the newcomers, there was a mix of triumph and crisis. Katarina Witt, skating to the music from *Robin Hood*, delivered a precise technical program, but her marks got her no higher than sixth place. That was one rung below Germany's young Tanya Szewczenko who was being hailed as the next Katarina. China's Lu Chen surprised by taking fourth spot. And for Surya Bonaly, she of the spectacular jumps, it was third place. Just ahead of her, in second place, was Oksana Baiul, the sixteen-year-old orphan from the Ukraine who had been a complete unknown two years earlier. On this night in Northern Lights Hall, performing a Black Swan routine, Oksana delivered an exceptional show. She double-footed a triple-Lutz jump, but

106

that was her single flaw, and with the highest marks of the evening for presentation, she got second place on solid merit.

Which brings us to the large names of the evening, Harding and Kerrigan. In the case of one, Harding, it was strictly anti-climax. She skated a program that placed her way down the list, number ten and out of the running for medals. So much for Tonya Harding. With Nancy Kerrigan it was all emotion, balance and gorgeous skating. It was hard to believe that this was her first performance in competition since the attack on her in January. She came close to perfection, landing all her elements, earning first place ordinals from seven judges, bringing the crowd to its feet in a terrific display of enthusiasm. Everyone cheered, everyone clapped. Even Tonya Harding clapped. She sat in a private box high up in the hall and, caught by the cameras, she applauded Nancy Kerrigan. It was just that Harding's applause didn't look quite as enthusiastic as everyone else's.

Ordinals
When the judges marks for figure skating are posted many fans miss the most important ingredient, the ordinal. Ordinals indicate where the skater is ranked in relation to the others who have already skated. It becomes the determining factor in the final standings.

DAY THIRTEEN

A GREAT DAY FOR FLYING

Thursday, February 24, 1994

Here, very roughly, is what happens in a freestyle skiing aerial competition: the skier bolts down a sharp incline, flies over a huge jump, and in the the air, in a few seconds, performs all manner of acrobatics, body-defying moves like a triple back somersault with three full twists, or, in the language of the hill, a triple, back, full, full, full. That accomplished, the skier comes back to earth, landing on his skis and looking entirely unperturbed.

Going into the aerials medal competition at the Kanthaugen Freestyle Arena, Canada happened to have some athletes who could handle this daredevil sport better than anyone in the world. One was Philippe LaRoche. All Philippe had accomplished was to win the world title in 1991, the gold at Albertville where the aerial event was still a demonstration sport, and the world championship again

in 1993. Then there was Lloyd Langlois. He reigned as the current World Cup Grand Prix champion, but if you asked Lloyd about motivation just before the Games, he would have mentioned Naomi. She was Lloyd's brand new baby daughter, and he intended to win a medal for her.

But neither Lloyd nor Philippe, nor anyone else, had quite counted on Andreas "Sonny" Schonbachler. He was a Swiss aerialist, a veteran at the sport, and he announced that the Olympic competition would mark his farewell to the world of aerials. It was his last jump, and it was a honey. He knew he'd pulled off something remarkable when he landed. He yanked off his helmet and sent it spiralling into the air. Then he settled back to watch the Canadians, defying them to beat the marks he had just racked up.

Lloyd Langlois tried first. As Lloyd prepared to launch into his jump, the sound system was playing the old Presley tune, *Don't Be Cruel*. Was this some sort of symbolism? Lloyd performed the triple-twisting triple. That's three twists and three somersaults in the air. Lloyd looked great and landed perfectly. There was just one problem—the judges marked him below Sonny Schonbachler.

The last jumper, the last man to take a run at Schonbachler, was Philippe LaRoche. He raced down the incline, soared off the kicker, and hurled himself into one of those moves they call the full, full, full. It's one of the most difficult jumps in the sport, and Philippe handled it beautifully. If there was a flaw, it might have been in his slightly rough landing, and that could have accounted for the judges' reaction. They placed Philippe

just ahead of Lloyd Langlois, but just behind Sonny Schonbachler. It was gold for Schonbachler on the last jump of his career, silver and bronze for the two Canadians.

In fact, of the top six finishers in the men's aerials, Canada had four placings, with Andy Capicik getting fourth and Nicolas Fontaine grabbing sixth. And just to round out the aerials picture, Canada's Caroline Olivier scored a respectable eighth in the women's competition.

For one woman, Day Thirteen brought the end of a remarkable chase. This was Lyubov Egorova, the indefatigable cross-country skier from Russia. She had won a gold or silver medal in nine straight Olympic races over her career. If she brought her total to ten, she would equal the all-time mark for medals won which was held by her former Russian teammate Raisa Smetanina. More than that,

Egorova had six career golds, one short of a new Olympic record. And today, Day Thirteen, in the tough 30 km race, Egorova had her chance to make or equal a piece of history. Alas, history struck back. Egorova's valiant race got her only up to fifth place. But when one streak ends, another begins, and the winner of the 30 km was Manuela Di Centa of Italy who captured her fifth medal and second gold of the Games.

On this night, it was back to the Northern Lights Hall in Hamar, back to short track speedskating, back to the event that guaranteed thrills, controversy and sometimes, confusion. The feature was the women's 500 m, and that would bring the Canadians up against Cathy Turner, the American whose collision with Sylvie Daigle at the Albertville 500 m knocked Sylvie out of the race while Turner skated to the gold.

Love Turner or loathe her—most Canadian skaters leaned to the latter point of view— she had a *curriculum vitae* that was a genuine attention grabber. She started as a promising long track speedskater, training with Bonnie Blair in the late 1970s. But, she decided in 1980 that the life of a world class athlete wasn't all it was cracked up to be, and she made a monumental career shift—into show business. She worked lounges as a singer-songwriter. At the same time, she dabbled with computers, earned a blue belt in tae-kwon-do, got into ski racing, and won championships in cycling and water-skiing. And did I mention her skate race against Al Iafrate? That's Al Iafrate, the star NHL defenceman noted for his speed. Turner beat him in the race. That isn't all. After her foray into short track racing, after she won the gold at the '92 Olympics, she, typical Turner, quit

Facing page
Cathy Turner takes
gold.

This page
The Danger Zone—
Nathalie Lambert and
Cathy Turner.

the sport and toured with the *Ice Capades*. Now she was back to the short track, back for another try at Olympic gold.

She was also back to her old trick of annoying the Canadians. In the 500 m quarter-finals, Turner and Canada's Nathalie Lambert came up against one another. The two were racing neck and neck when Turner tried to pass Lambert on the outside. The two women's skates locked, and it was Nathalie who fell in a heap. Turner remained upright and advanced to the semi-finals. Nathalie was out of the competition, and she was furious.

"[Turner's] been getting away with this for years and keeps getting away with it," Nathalie said. "She skates like she owns the ice. She's really dirty. She makes our sport look like roller derby."

It wasn't Turner who brought down Sylvie Daigle in her quarter-final. Sylvie was taken out in a fall with the Russian skater, Marina Pylaeva, and both women found themselves disqualified. But it was Turner, in one semi-final, who contributed to the disqualification of the last of the Canadian racers, Isabelle Charest.

Isabelle went into the race with words of caution about Turner from Sylvie and Nathalie. That may have turned into a negative for Isabelle. Perhaps she was too conscious of Turner, perhaps too intent on taking a taste of revenge. Whatever was on Isabelle's mind, the key episode began to unfold on one of the corners when Turner tried to slip inside. Charest fought to hold her line. But she couldn't and in the collision that followed, Isabelle took down both Turner and Hye-Kyung Won of South Korea. When the judges sorted out the mess, they allowed Turner, Hye-Kyung Won and the third of the

four skaters in that semi-final heat to do a reskate. They disqualified Isabelle, and in the reskate, Turner and the South Korean advanced to the final.

Turner, even without any Canadians around to harass, generated more controversy in the final. It was a race in which elbows were flying, and one of the other skaters, China's Yanmei Zhang, no stranger herself to rough and tumble tactics, kept indicating by her body language that Turner was interfering with her. At one point, mid-race, Zhang threw up her hands in disgust. Turner barrelled ahead, and with a last burst, she crossed the finish line in first place with a disgusted Zhang in second and another American, Amy Peterson, in third.

That set the stage for more antics at the presentation ceremony. Zhang stood stolidly on the podium, refusing to acknowledge the presence of the two Americans, Turner and Peterson, and when the last notes of the U.S. national anthem died away, Zhang unleashed her temper for all the world to marvel at. Or at least, the part of the world that caught the dead-on work of CTV cameraman, Don Metz, who recorded Zhang in full flight as she stormed from the podium, took off her silver medal, flung her flowers to the ice and stomped toward the dressing room. That's where someone intercepted Zhang, someone who consoled Zhang, someone who knew exactly how Zhang felt. That person offering consolation was Canada's Nathalie Lambert.

As for Cathy Turner, the gold medalist, we got her version of events and of her own style in a quick live interview at ice level.

"I don't know why everybody's mad at me," she told us. "I'm just tough out there. That's the way I skate. I don't consider myself

dirty. I consider myself a fighter. If I had done something wrong, I would've been disqualified."

I asked her what lay in her future plans. More singing? Back to the *Ice Capades*?

Turner's answer couldn't have been sweeter.

"I just want to enjoy this," she said. "I'm the happiest person in the world right now. I just want to celebrate with my husband."

The women figure skaters wouldn't be in action until Friday night's free skate, but Day Thirteen still brought a development that could be key to the gold medal. It seemed that during practice in Hamar, Oksana Baiul and Germany's Tanja Szewczenko got them-

selves launched on a collision course. Both were skating backwards, setting up for jumps, when they caught sight of one another. But...too late. Szewczenko emerged from the crash winded and with a bruised elbow. Baiul's injury was more serious. Her own skate had gashed her lower right leg. The cut took three stitches to close. Pain in her lower back bothered her too, and the early worry was that she might not be in skating condition by Friday night. The good news was that the incident took the Harding-Kerrigan saga out of the headlines. The bad news was that a freak accident could end a gifted young woman's challenge for gold.

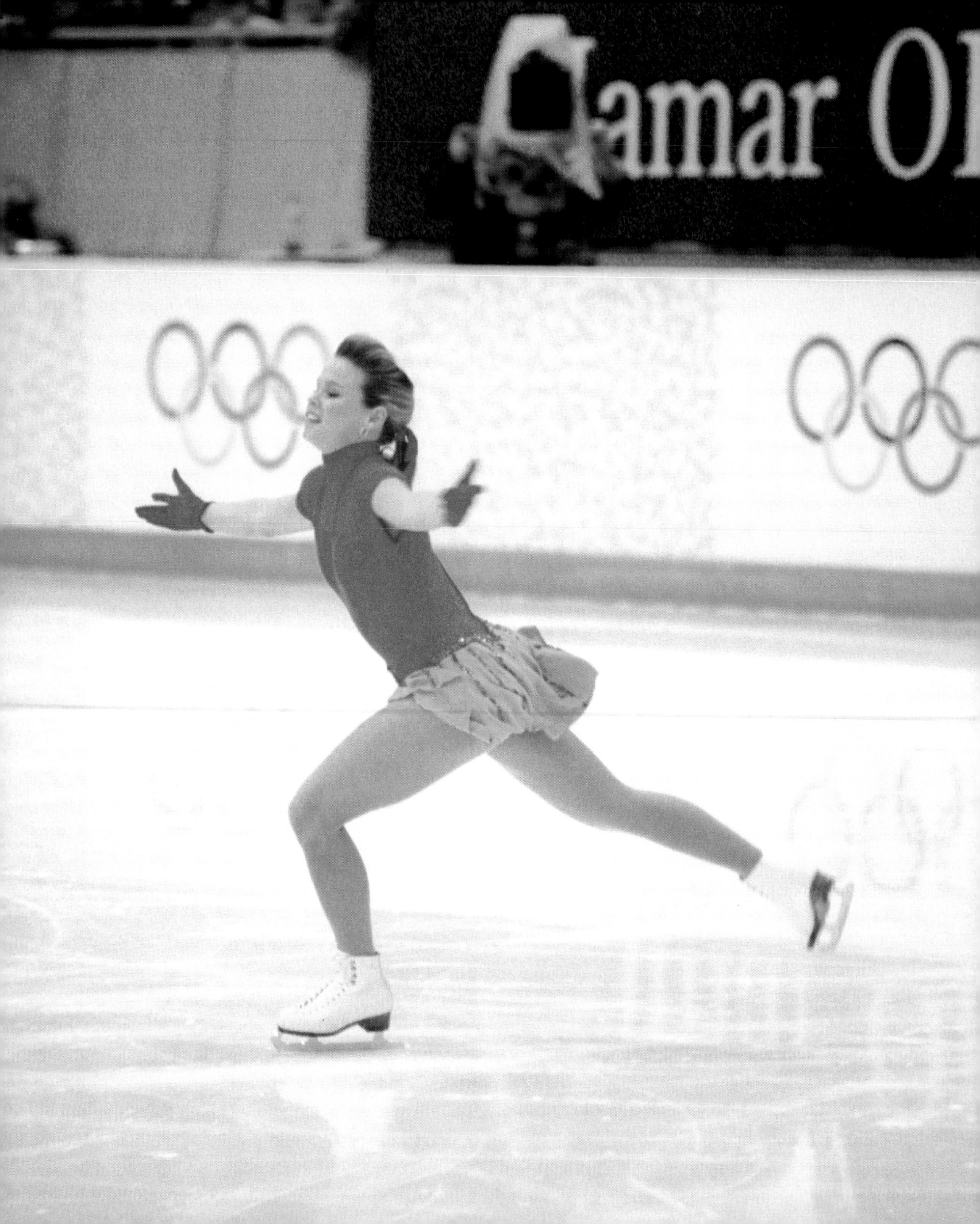
amar O

DAY FOURTEEN

A LITTLE DESTINY

Friday, February 25, 1994

This was to be a day of major encounters.

In hockey, it was Canada versus Finland in one semi-final, Russia against Sweden in the other. On the figure skating ice, the showdown would bring Nancy Kerrigan and Oksana Baiul—if she was fit to skate—into the limelight. And in the big picture, in the contest between all nations for the most medals won at the Games, it was shaping up as a battle between Germany and the host country, Norway.

The hosts were three medals up on the Germans, twenty to seventeen, as the day began. Germany got one back on the biathlon range, placing second in the women's 4 x 7.5 km relay (Russia won with France getting the bronze. Canada came in fifteenth with the loudest ovation of the entire competition saved for the Canadian star of the circuit, Myriam Bédard). But Norway increased its lead by a

medal in the K90 ski jumping when the home country's Espen Bredesen won gold, his teammate Lasse Ottesen got silver, while Germany's Dieter Thoma slipped in for bronze. When Germany dominated the women's 5000 m speedskating at the Viking Ship in Hamar with Claudia Pechstein and Gunda Niemann running one, two (Japan's Hiromi Yamamoto came third), the total stood at 22 medals for Norway, 21 for Germany, and it was time for one of the two countries to make a serious move.

The country that moved—a very big-time move—was Norway, and the sport they chose to move on was the slalom half of the men's combined alpine. Not since 1956 had one country swept all three medals in a men's alpine event; that year, Toni Sailer led a one-two-three finish for Austria. In 1994, it was about to happen again when three joyous Norwegians, Lasse Kjus, Kjetil Andre

117

*This page
Tonya Harding's lace
breaks as her pro-
gram begins.*

Aamodt and Harald Strand Nillsen hurtled down the slalom course to gold, silver and bronze. At the presentation ceremonies, the three skiers leaped off the podium and celebrated with an *élan* I'd never seen at any other Olympic medal presentation. Each medalist grabbed a partner and with Norwegian music striking up, they set off on a brilliant, happy jig full of bubbling good spirits. As much as any single incident at these Olympics, this victory dance captured the wonderful essence of the Lillehammer Games.

In the evening, at the hall in Hamar, the first moment of high drama—or was it low melodrama?—came when the eighth skater had just begun her routine. The skater suddenly stopped the program. She was standing at the far end of the ice, and she was no longer skating. What was it? A missed jump? An injury? Something else? All we knew in

that instant was that the halt in the routine meant trouble for someone. The skater was Tonya Harding.

She stood still on the ice. Then, the tears starting to come, she skated to the head judge's position at the side of the arena. It seemed that Harding had broken a skate lace. She was asking for time to fix the lace and to take a reskate later in her flight. This was a familiar story with Harding. At the 1993 U.S. Nationals, a strap in her dress had snapped, and at the 1993 Skate America, one of her skate blades had come loose. In each case, she was permitted a reskate. That's what happened again, here at the Olympics, a reskate.

Who was the unfortunate victim of the whole incident?

Josée Chouinard of Canada.

With Harding granted a reprieve, Josée was forced to skate immediately, three minutes

earlier than she had planned, three minutes earlier than the schedule stated. Was this such a big deal? Sure it was. Josée was backstage, preparing herself mentally, physically, psychologically for the biggest performance of her life, and out of the blue, she was told, you're on, kid!

Josée admitted to us later that the rush had caught her off stride. And the surprise—the slight degree of unpreparedness that was forced on her—showed when she fell on her first attempted triple. She picked up her routine from that point, but she fell again at the end. As she came off the ice and sat in the kiss-and-cry area, there was a look of utter disbelief. She and her coach, Louis Stong, said nothing to one another. They sat and stared at the marks. Those marks would ultimately place Josée in ninth place. Had she once again succumbed to the pressure of interna-

tional competition? Or was it the plain rotten bad luck to be forced to the ice when Tonya Harding abandoned it?

Harding finally made her appearance. Scattered boos greeted her. Maybe people were tired of the Tonya Harding story. Maybe they just wished she'd go away. Harding performed her routine, and in many ways, given the circumstances of the glare of publicity that had followed her for weeks, she did a brave job of it. She landed four solid triples, and at the end of her skate, she pumped her fist in the air. Her performance got her eighth place.

Backstage, she told us that she couldn't believe her lace had broken. She said, somewhat darkly, that maybe someone just didn't want her to skate. As she started to walk away from us, into the mob of microphones waiting behind me, I asked a final question. Was it all worth it, everything she had gone through?

Facing page
Oksana Baiul, ban-
daged and exultant.

This page
Scenes from Oksana
Baiul's gold medal-
winning program.

She stared back at me, a steely gaze in her blue eyes, and she answered in one word, "Definitely."

Back on the ice, China's Lu Chen restored the spirit of competition. She completed six triple jumps, and briefly topped the leader board. She was spectacular, solid and safe.

Kerrigan, knowing what was asked of her, skated to a medley of Neil Diamond songs, and hit a small glitch at the very beginning of her routine. She doubled her opening triple jump. But the rest of her routine was an exercise in the ideal. She missed nothing, and she wowed the crowd, drawing a standing ovation at the end of her performance. Kerrigan was first, Lu Chen second.

The word was that Oksana Baiul would skate. She had stitches, she had bruising, she had a sore back. She may even have had shaky nerves. But there was no sign of disabilities when she took to the ice. She landed five triples, she captivated the crowd with her ballerina-like style, she seemed to spread positive impressions all around her. The skate wasn't perfect, but it demonstrated that Baiul possessed tremendous inner strength. She fought for everything, and when the judges showed their marks, Baiul, sitting in the kiss-and-cry area, registered an emotion that looked like shock. The marks meant she had the gold.

A bruised Tanja Szewczenko was still to skate. Hurting from her collision with Baiul didn't make this her easiest skate or her best performance. She would finish sixth.

France's Surya Bonaly was the next to last skater. She had all the jumps, but couldn't artistically impress the judges. She looked uncomfortable from the start, and the judges marked her down to fourth.

This page and next
Katarina Witt
returned to these
Olympics after
skating as a pro.

The last skater of the night had no chance at gold, but Katarina Witt won the audience over with her routine to the song, *Where Have All the Flowers Gone?*. It was a tribute to the people of Sarajevo where she had won the first of her two Olympic golds in 1984. Witt would eventually place seventh.

Nancy Kerrigan had her own thoughts about who should have won the gold. "I was clean," she said afterwards. "Oksana wasn't. I didn't have any touchdowns, didn't make any mistakes." The judges disagreed. When all the marks were in, Baiul edged Kerrigan by a single judge. So it was gold for Baiul, the orphan from the Ukraine, silver for a highly disappointed Kerrigan, and bronze, the first winter Olympics medal ever won by a Chinese athlete, for Lu Chen.

A few minutes later, as the skaters prepared for the medal ceremony, Lu Chen and

Nancy Kerrigan waited, impatiently on Kerrigan's part, for the gold medalist. Baiul was still in the dressing room. Chen and Kerrigan happened to be doing their waiting beside our broadcast position, and Kerrigan asked me a logical question.

"What's going on?"

I told her two things, that Baiul hadn't come out of the dressing room yet, and that officials were trying to find a recording of the Ukrainian national anthem.

"Oh, what's the difference?" Kerrigan snapped. "She's just going to come out here and cry anyway."

What Kerrigan didn't realize was that the two of us were standing in front of a live camera that caught her infelicitous crack. It was clear that Kerrigan was understandably reacting to the horrendous pressure she had lived under for weeks. But it was also clear

that she'd better try a little damage control, something to enhance her image after the remark about Baiul.

"It's been a circus," Kerrigan said. "I've felt like I've been in prison. I can't wait to get back home and get on with my life."

Baiul finally put in an appearance. She was crying. And she cried all the way through the playing of her country's new anthem.

Victor Tikhonov didn't imitate a kangaroo or a jumping jack on this day. No dancing by the Russian hockey coach, no hugging his assistant coaches, no broad grins. Russia lost. The final score was Sweden 4, Russia 3. But the score flattered Russia. The Swedes jumped out to a fast 2–0 lead on goals by Magnus Svensson and Patrik Juhlin, and stayed in front all the way until, with Sweden leading 4–1 in the waning seconds of the game, Russia popped two goals that

saved face but not the game. Sweden moved to the gold medal game.

The other semi-final game, the one that all Canadians had their hopes pinned on was Canada versus Finland. After a scoreless first period, it was the Finns who put the Canadians deep in a hole with two fast goals from Saku Kolvu and Esa Keskinen early in the second period.

This was a Finnish team that came into the Games beautifully prepared. They had chosen to get ready for the Olympics by sticking to their home base. They worked at home, avoided the rigors of a pre-Olympic schedule, and persuaded a share of players with NHL experience to beef up the team. At the start of the Games, the Finns constituted something of an unknown quantity, but after steaming through the round robin and the quarter-finals without a loss, they stood revealed as a tough, capable squad.

Our Canadians had their own share of toughness, and in the second period, Todd Hlushko and Petr Nedved got the goals that tied the game. The teams fought into the third period, and it was then that a player who had been among the very last to join the Canadians, someone who turned out to be a final piece in the team puzzle, asserted himself. He was Brad Werenka, an Edmonton Oiler defenceman, and on the key third-period play, he cheated into the slot at Finland's end. Greg Johnson, wearing a face mask to protect the nose he'd shattered in the Czechoslovakia game, spotted Werenka's move. Johnson passed the puck and Werenka smacked a one-timer behind Jukka Tammi, the Finn goaltender.

Jean-Yves Roy made it 4–2 Canada. Greg Parks, playing with an injured rib, scored another to make it 5–2. The Finns added a late tally but when the final seconds ticked off the clock, the dream had come a little bit closer.

The players poured over the bench. Corey Hirsch was mobbed. Canada was going back to the gold medal game. They would finish no worse than silver. On the ice, Greg Therrien and Adrian Aucoin danced in each other's arms. Tom Renney and Dany Dubé enjoyed the scene and Brad Werenka soaked it all in.

"It was pretty quick, me coming here. Ever since I saw the U.S. team win in 1980 it's been a dream of mine to be here. It hasn't been hard to get the fever."

Corey Hirsch relished another meeting with Sweden in the final. "We're going to do the same thing we've been doing. Heart, character, and desire. That's what we're about and that's why we're going for gold."

The Net-cam

Doug Beeforth, CTV's Director of Sports, was inspired by an old hockey picture in Sports Illustrated that showed a spectacular shot, at the perfect angle, of the action in the goaltender's crease. Why couldn't that be shown on TV? After months of experimentation, Beeforth's concept became reality in Lillehammer when the net-cam made its debut. Affixed inside the goal net, the remote-controlled camera gave a panoramic view from behind the goalkeeper. It scored big with viewers and set a new standard for television hockey coverage.

DAY FIFTEEN

CLASS

Saturday, February 26, 1994

What I'll remember most from Day Fifteen is the class shown by a couple of Canadian athletes. It was a day of exciting events, vivid performances, big-name athletes shining in their specialities. But none of those people or performances will dislodge from my memory two people who didn't win.

Vreni Schneider won. She took gold in the women's slalom, and since she'd also been the gold medalist for Switzerland in the slalom and giant slalom at the 1988 Calgary Games, she became the first woman ever to win three golds in alpine skiing. Finland was a winner in hockey. The Finns took the bronze medal when they shut out Russia, 4–0. And in the men's 4 x 7.5 km relay biathlon, the German team won by an extraordinary margin. The German anchor man, Sven Fischer, was so far out in front of the second-place Russian and the third-place French biathlete that when he entered the stadium on the final lap he had time to mingle with German fans who handed him a huge flag to carry across the finish line.

The first Canadian to stick in my mind from Day Fifteen's competition was Chris Lori in the four-man bobsled.

Both Canadian drivers, Lori and Pierre Lueders, came into the four-man after disappointments in the two-man competition. But both came into today's first of two days of four-man racing with strong crews.

Pierre's sled relied on size and strength. Pierre was himself a big man, and so were the other men on his sled, brakeman Dave MacEachern (the only Prince Edward Islander at the Games), Pascal Caron and Jack Pyc (a pair of 21-year-olds). They had power, and they had Pierre's brash, confident, even arrogant style.

This page, and next
Nathalie Lambert
skates to a silver
medal.

Chris Lori's sled was more of a speed-and-finesse operation. Glenroy Gilbert, the world-class sprinter on the track in summertime, was the brakeman, and the other two members of the team, Sheridon Baptiste and Chris Farstad, were great for swift acceleration.

So, who would challenge for a medal, the crew with the power or the crew with the speed?

The answer was neither. Chris Lori's sled finished the day in ninth place while Pierre Lueder was even further back, in thirteenth place. Their chances for a medal had dwindled to almost nil.

But Chris Lori's defeat wasn't what stuck in my mind about the man. Instead, I remember his visit to our studio earlier in the week. He'd already made a disappointing couple of runs in the two-man bobsled. But in the studio, it wasn't disappointment or

defeat he wanted to share with us. It was the hundreds of letters he'd received from children back home in Windsor, Ontario. The kids were important to Chris. He was the man who returned home from Albertville in 1992 downhearted at missing a bronze medal by ten-hundredths of a second. He found himself greeted at the airport by a youngster in a wheelchair holding a sign that read "Congratulations, Chris." That, Chris said, put Olympic medals in perspective. There were more significant things in life, and one of them, Chris told us in the TV studio in Lillehammer, was to answer all the children's letters he'd received, to give the kids someone to look up to.

To me, Chris Lori was a man for children to look up to, an example for us all.

So was Stephen Gough. He was a member of Canada's 5000 m relay team in short track

speedskating, and he was another who didn't allow defeat to crush his best instincts.

Before this final night of short track speed-skating began, the officials of the International Skating Union and the International Olympic Committee had joined forces to bring some order to the wild and crazy antics that had marked the earlier races. The officials got serious. They got so serious that in the women's 1000 m race, they disqualified Cathy Turner.

Whether or not it was her absence, the 1000 m final developed into a sensational race. And Nathalie Lambert was in the thick of the action (Sylvie Daigle had been disqualified in her semi-final and Isabelle Charest had finished third in hers). Nathalie wasn't in possession of her full power because the collision with Turner in the 500 m quarter-finals had left her with pain in one knee. But she

ignored the ache, focussed on the race, and stormed down the stretch neck and neck and neck with two Koreans, Chun Lee-Kyung and Kim So-Hee. When the three women hit the finish line, Nathalie had sandwiched herself in the middle, gold for Chun, bronze for Kim, and silver for Nathalie Lambert.

Canada's male short track speedskaters couldn't match Nathalie's feat on this day. In the 500 metres, Derrick Campbell crashed out of his quarter-final heat, Freddie Blackburn finished fifth in one semi-final, and only Marc Gagnon made it through to the finals. That's where he faltered. Marc is on most occasions a steady, smart, relentless skater, but on this occasion, he came around a corner and lost an edge. He was out of contention as Korea's Chae Ji-Hoon skated to gold.

The men had one last shot at a medal in the 5000 m relay. They'd won a silver medal

in the event at Albertville, and in this year's final against teams from the U.S., Italy and Australia, they seemed a shoe-in for a medal. Canada got away strongly and was holding position. Then Stephen Gough made his error. Stephen was the rookie, a 24-year-old from Fredericton, and new to the team. And, going low into a corner, he lost his balance. He went down, slid into a padded wall, and by the time he recovered and tagged off to a teammate, Canada had fallen far behind. They skated hard for the rest of the 5000 m, hoping at least one of the other teams would falter. But none of them did. Italy took the gold, the U.S. got the silver, and the bronze went to the Aussies who celebrated their country's first ever Winter Olympic medal by breaking into a rousing rendition of *Waltzing Matilda.*

That's when Stephen Gough showed what he's made of. He didn't have to appear on TV. He didn't have to do an interview. But Stephen, on his own, unbidden, headed straight for our interview area. He spoke into the camera. He made no excuses. He accepted blame for his fall. And he said he wouldn't let the slip ruin his life. The young man was only 24, but to me, he came across as admirably mature. He carried himself, as Chris Lori had earlier, like a man with class.

DAY SIXTEEN

*Facing page
Young fans getting
ready for some
"rockin' at Hakan."*

HEADS HELD HIGH

Sunday, February 27

It's always the same. The last day of the Games feels strange. It's that way for all of us, athletes, coaches, spectators, hosts, media. We've worked hard, all of us in our different ways, and we've experienced the tremendous joy and excitement of great sport. But now it's winding down, and it feels strange.

Four events were left: the four-man bobsled, the men's slalom, the 50 km cross-country classic and—the one that had all Canadians caught in high anticipation—the hockey final.

Harald Czudaj for Germany steered his sled to gold in the four-man bobsled in a competition that, for Canada, ended with Chris Lori's team dropping back to eleventh place and Pierre Lueders' team improving to twelfth. Vladimir Smirnov of Kazakhstan, after ten years of competition at the Olympics, ten years as a superb cross-country skier, won his first medal in the sport, a gold

that the huge, appreciative crowd hailed with a tumultuous cheer. And at Hafjell in the men's slalom, the gold went to Thomas Stangassinger of Austria. Most of the cheers were saved for the silver medal winner, Italy's mighty Alberto Tomba. Ski critics had been hammering Tomba for most of the season, claiming that he was over the hill, no longer a contender. But the irrepressible Tomba proved he had at least one more splendid race left in him, and his silver medal gave him a career total of three golds and two silvers, the most ever in Olympic alpine history.

At Hakan Hall, Don Chevrier came on air for CTV and said, "They're rockin' at Hakan!"

The crowd that filled every space in the hall was easily the most boisterous of the Games. Half the people wore red and white for Canada—a group that included Kurt Browning, Myriam Bédard, Jean-Luc

---

Alberto Tomba

Italy's "La Bomba" burst onto the world stage in Calgary where he won gold medals in both the slalom and giant slalom events. The ski hill playboy always attracts a crowd and always entertains. In Albertville, he won gold in the giant slalom and silver in the slalom. He celebrated his Lillehammer slalom silver with a back flip— and a cappuccino.

133

*This page and next
The game for gold:
Canada vs Sweden.*

Hockey

The first rules for hockey specifying use of a puck were laid down in 1837. Halifax, Montréal, Kingston and Windsor were all homes to early teams and games. Ice hockey made its Olympic debut in 1920, at the Summer Games held in Antwerp. Olympic hockey competition features 12 teams. They include the host country, the defending Olympic champion and teams picked from last year's World Championships. These teams are divided into pools of six teams each which play a round robin tournament. The best four from each pool advance to an elimination round to determine the final standings.

Brassard and all the other hockey fans among our Olympic athletes—and the other half had on the yellow and blue for Sweden. The place throbbed with the thrill of what was to come, and from where I was standing, I could almost grab the tension in the air. Where was I standing? In the area squarely between the two opposing team's benches. Best spot in the house.

Earlier, I'd been down below, chatting with the Canadian players in the corridor, checking out the walking wounded. There were plenty of those. Mark Astley had a bashed ankle that would have prevented most people from taking a step. He intended to play hockey on that ankle. The same went for Greg Parks; he'd play with a banged-up rib. And Greg Johnson's face—multiple stitches, broken nose—made him look like a living Halloween mask. But he'd play.

The spirit of these young men was something to marvel at. They'd come from every hockey background to play for Canada. Some, like Petr Nedved, were proven NHLers. Some—19-year-old Paul Kariya—were stars in the making. Some—Fabian Joseph, Wally Schreiber, Brad Schlegel—had played for our Olympic team at the Albertville Games. But all, no matter what disparate route brought them to Hakan Hall on this afternoon, were motivated by one consuming objective: to bring the hockey gold home to Canada.

Speaking of motivators, the Canadian dressing room had plenty of them. There were goodwill faxes pasted to the wall, messages from former players, from kids in Canada, from Wayne Gretzky, from the members of the Edmonton Mercuries.

On the team bench, there was a particular symbol that spoke of these players'

 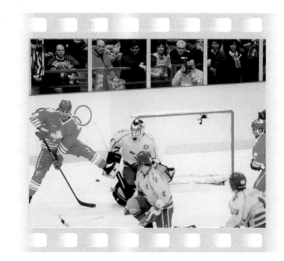

togetherness. It was a hockey stick bearing the names of all the players who had at one time been members of the team. Some had been cut. Some had moved on. Some—Brett Lindros was one of these—had been taken away by injury. Dany Dubé, the assistant coach, held the stick for me and explained, "Every one of these guys on the stick is part of all of this today."

Out on the ice, even during the warm-up before the game, an added piece of drama touched the Canadian team. Manny Legace, the back-up goalie, was injured. A puck caught him in the small area between the top of his pads and the lower part of his hockey pants. He was in severe pain, but, even on crutches, there was no way he would watch this game from anywhere except the team bench. Todd Warriner was on the bench too, in uniform. There wasn't a chance in the whole wide world that Todd could play. He'd

suffered strained knee ligaments in an earlier game, but in a generous move, coach Tom Renney invited Todd to suit up for the big game. Todd had earned the right to be part of whatever was to come, gold or silver.

From the drop of the first puck in the first period, this turned into a game of classic hockey. It was a game of speed, grace and toughness. Sweden probably had the edge in pure puck-handling and passing skills. But Canada took the advantage in hard-nosed and unforgiving determination. Overall the Swedish finesse may have dominated. That showed up in the shots on goal; the Swedes had 42 of them over regulation time to just half that many, 21, for the Canadians. But by the same token, Corey Hirsch gave the edge to Canada in goaltending, stopping forty shots to nineteen for Tommy Salo of Sweden. No matter what the statistics indicated, the

Hakan Hall
The larger of the two venues, Hakan Hall seats 10,500 for hockey. It is located just 3 km from the Lillehammer Olympic Village.

135

level of hockey remained absolutely brilliant at all times. There was no stalling in this game, no tentativeness, no goon stuff, just hockey the way it was meant to be played.

In the first period, Canada's Mark Astley was whistled for a hooking penalty. This was at 5:44, and 26 seconds later, Tomas Jonsson, the former New York Islander defenceman, banged a shot past Hirsch after a pretty passing play with Hakan Loob and Peter Forsberg. The game stayed that way, 1–0 Sweden, through the rest of the first period, through the second when Corey Hirsch did everything but stand on his head in making sixteen saves, and into the third when Canada finally struck back. The time was 9.08 when Paul Kariya tipped a Greg Johnson shot behind Tommy Salo. That tied the game.

But it stayed that way for only two minutes and 25 seconds, which was how long it took for Derek Mayer to pull off a terrific, individual piece of hockey work. Derek was a young guy from Rossland, B.C., home of Nancy Greene and Kerrin-Lee Gartner. He had started out with the National/Olympic program in 1989, then quit it to turn pro in the Detroit Red Wing organization. He realized his heart remained with the Olympic team and returned in time to contribute to the great Lillehammer adventure. His contribution in the third period, with 8:17 left in the game, was a sweet unassisted goal that put Canada in front for the first time, 2–1.

Throughout the entire third period, a period of tough but clean hockey, the referee had not called a single penalty. That changed at 17:50. A penalty! The only penalty, as it would turn out, of the period. It was whistled against Brad Werenka for holding. Sweden had been coming hard at Canada all through

the third. Now, with a man advantage, they stepped up the pace. Their passing plays were picture perfect, and one of them, Jonsson to Forsberg to Magnus Svensson set Svensson free to drill in the tying goal.

The game went into overtime.

The ten minutes of sudden-death overtime produced a couple of solid chances for both teams. Neither squad turned the chances into goals. It produced more stunning work from the two goalies. And it produced a moment of sweet retribution for Todd Hlushko. In the third, Magnus Svensson had caught Todd with his head down and levelled him with a check that gave Todd a bruised cheek and a fit of wooziness. Now, in overtime, a revived Todd crushed Sweden's Kenny Jonsson against the boards. Touché! Canada, Todd was announcing, wouldn't back down. The check infuriated Sweden's coach Bjom Lundmark

who screamed profanities at Tom Renney. But the confrontation faded away. So did the regulation overtime, and the game was headed to the dreaded and controversial shootout.

Under the rules, each team designated five shooters. Those five took turns, alternating, first one team, then the other, at the opposition goalie. Whichever team scored the most in the least number of shots—an unbeatable 4–2 margin, for example, or 4–3—won the game, not to mention the gold medal. If, at the end of the round of five, the score remained tied, then the shootout began again with a different set of shooters, except that, this time, the first team to score a goal, with the other team remaining scoreless on an equal number of shots, emerged the winner.

This was a recipe for heightened tension.

Canada won the coin toss and shot first. Petr Nedved was the shooter. He elected for

a wrist shot high to the corner. He scored. 1–0 Canada.

Haakan Loob for Sweden, the former Calgary Flame, aimed for the five hole. The shot didn't work. Still 1–0 Canada.

Paul Kariya followed Nedved's early example and shot high. The puck bounced off Tommy Salo's shoulder and into the net. 2–0 Canada.

Magnus Svensson made a terrific deke that sent Corey Hirsch sprawling. Svensson lifted the puck over Corey. 2–1 Canada.

Dwayne Norris tried a deke on Salo. Nothing wrong with the deke, except that Salo, down and out, made the save. 2–1 Canada.

Mats Naslund, 34 years old, a former Montreal Canadien, a senior hockey citizen at these Games, forced a shot off his backhand and went wide. 2–1 Canada.

Greg Parks, wearing a flak jacket to protect his injured rib, couldn't fool Salo. 2–1 Canada.

Peter Forsberg, the young star headed for the Québec Nordiques, showed a deke one way and shot a backhand the other way. The puck got past Hirsch. 2–2 tie.

Greg Johnson went for a quick shot in the slot. Salo was ready with the save. 2–2 tie.

Roger Hannson had a chance to wrap it up for Sweden. He tried a deke on Hirsch, but Corey, under terrific pressure, had Hannson in his sights all the way. The big save ended the first round of shootouts in a 2–2 tie.

Now it was sudden death, one goal for the game, one goal for the gold.

Sweden went first. Magnus Svensson was the shooter. This looked dangerous. Svensson had already scored twice this afternoon, once in regulation time, once in the shootout. Would he produce an unorthodox hat trick? Not this time. Corey Hirsch produced the big save.

Dream Teams
It appears the NHL will take an active role in the Olympic movement in the future and help stockpile "Dream Teams." Some like the idea; others don't. If you ask Tom Renney, he'll tell you they don't need millionaire NHLers in the Olympics. "Look at Lillehammer," Renney said, "We had our own Dream Team."

Petr Nedved, next up for Canada, could win it all. He put a nice deke on Salo that left the net open, but Petr's shot, on his backhand, somehow rolled off the toe of his stick and went wide.

Peter Forsberg for Sweden. He cut towards Hirsch, feinted to his forehand, and then, coming almost to a dead halt on his skates, switched to his backhand and slipped the puck under Hirsch's glove. The puck rolled into the net. Goal for Sweden. Hirsch chased after the referee. Corey thought Forsberg had crossed into his crease on the goal. The referee waved him off, and the TV replay showed that Corey had been mistaken. Sweden was a goal away from gold.

Paul Kariya was the man on the spot. If he scored, Canada would remain alive. He skated in on Salo. Was time standing still or was that only an illusion? Kariya went for a high wrist shot. Why not? He'd scored on a similar sort of shot a few minutes earlier. But not this time. This time, Tommy Salo took the puck on his leg pad. There was no goal for Paul Kariya, no win for this gutsy team, no gold for Canada.

In all the emotion that followed—the Canadian team sitting in stunned silence on their bench, Paul Kariya propping his elbow on the boards and holding his face, Tom Renney and Dany Dubé giving each of their players an embrace of pride—I'll always remember my interview with Todd Hlushko.

Todd was the young man who had tried so hard to win the gold medal that he had promised to his dying father. That was on Todd's mind. I reminded him that his dad would be tremendously proud of the silver. Todd had tears in his eyes, and some people who saw the interview said later that it might not have been proper to talk of this

subject at such a time. Those people don't know Todd. For Todd, his father had been with him in spirit through the entire Olympic quest, and what we had talked about on television, and the way we'd talked about it, was in a real sense a tribute to his dad. Todd was a young man of high character. And that's what was at the essence of the marvelous Canadian team. It may not have won gold. But it won our hearts and our respect.

At the Closing Ceremony that night, after the athletes had marched into the stadium, after the flag bearers from the different nations—Dan Jansen for the U.S., Philippe Candeloro for France, Myriam Bédard for Canada—formed a semi-circle around the rostrum, after the dignitaries took their places—two mayors stepped forward. One was from Lillehammer, Audun Tron, and the other,

Tasuku Tsukada, was from Nagano, Japan. They were about to take part in a ceremony that had begun at the Oslo Games in 1952. It's a ceremony in which the mayor of the Olympic Games just completed passes on a special Oslo flag to the mayor of the city which will next play host to the Games. In this case, Lillehammer was passing the flag to Nagano, Audun Tron to Tasuku Tsukada, and at the 1994 ceremony, Mayor Tron's words seemed strikingly contemporary, wise and appropriate.

"The Olympics are about sports and culture," he said. "Now, to the people of Lillehammer, the environment had become the third Olympic dimension. I know the city of Nagano will take care of the environment and do an even better job than we did."

There were other speeches, each of them intelligent and compassionate. Juan Antonio Samaranch's words had those qualities, espe-

cially coming from the man who was president of the International Olympic Committee.

"Ten years ago we gathered in Sarajevo," he said. "After much violence and many horrors, the situation there seems to be improving. Dear, dear Sarajevo, we do not forget you. We will keep supporting you."

Then Samaranch spoke the words designated in the Olympic charter.

"I declare the Seventeenth Olympic Games closed," he said, "and in accordance with tradition, I call upon the youth of the world to assemble four years from now at Nagano to celebrate there the Eighteenth Winter Games."

A fanfare sounded. The Olympic flame grew dimmer. And suddenly the stadium was alive with lights. They came from the flashlights that each person in the crowd had been given on the way into the stadium. The flashlights bore the inscription, "Remember Sarajevo."

The Olympic flame flickered and vanished. Simultaneously, the Olympic flag began its slow descent down the pole. At the bottom, attendants carried it out of the stadium. The flag bearers followed, and once they were clear of the gates, the sounds of the farewell song filled the stadium. It was over. The athletes together down below broke into hugs, cheers, tears, and, finally, at the very end, they danced in joy.

Looking across the stadium, feeling the exhilaration of it all, exhilaration for the Norwegians who had staged such a magnificent Games, for the Canadians who had won thirteen medals, the most ever for Canada, I watched something swirling in the air, something just a little bit different. It had begun at the moment the Olympic flame flickered out. It was snow. It was snowing for the first time in sixteen clear and luminous days at the Winter Olympic Games in Lillehammer.

Canada at Nagano
What about Canada's team for Nagano, Japan in 1998? Some of the younger athletes will return. Others, naturally, will go on to other things. We can look forward to the inclusion of two new official medal sports in which Canada excels-curling and women's hockey.

XVII

OLYMPIC WINTER GAMES

Official Canadian Team

Alpine Skiing
Rob Boyd
Rob Crossan
Thomas Grandi
Kerrin-Lee Gartner
Cary Mullen
Kate Pace
Edi Podivinsky
Michelle Ruthven
Luke Sauder
Ralf Socher
Brian Stemmle
Mélanie Turgeon

Biathlon
Myriam Bédard
Kristin Berg
Steve Cyr
Gillian Hamilton
Jane Isakson
Lise Meloche
Glenn Rupertus

Bobsleigh
Sheridon Baptiste
Mark Brus
Pascal Caron
Chris Farstad
Glenroy Gilbert
Chris Lori
Pierre Lueders
Dave MacEachern
Dennis Marineau
Jack Pyc
Guy Scheffer

Cross-country Skiing
Dany Bouchard

Freestyle Skiing
Jean-Luc Brassard
Andy Capicik
Nicolas Fontaine
Genevieve Fortin
Katherina Kubenk
Lloyd Langlois
Philippe LaRoche
Caroline Olivier
Kennedy Ryan
John Smart
Julie Steggall
Bronwen Thomas

Figure Skating
Shae-Lynn Bourne
Isabelle Brasseur
Sébastien Britten
Kurt Browning
Josée Chouinard
Lloyd Eisler
Susan Humphreys
Victor Kraatz
Jamie Salé
Kristy Sargeant
Elvis Stojko
Jason Turner
Kris Wirtz

Hockey
Mark Astley
Adrian Aucoin
David Harlock
Corey Hirsch
Todd Hlushko
Greg Johnson
Fabian Joseph
Paul Kariya
Chris Kontos
Manny Legace
Ken Lovsin
Derek Mayer
Petr Nedved
Dwayne Norris
Greg Parks
Alain Roy
Jean-Yves Roy
Brian Savage
Brad Schlegel
Wally Schreiber
Chris Therien
Todd Warriner
Brad Werenka

Luge
Bob Gasper
Clay Ives

Speedskating—Long Track
Susan Auch
Patrick Bouchard
Sylvain Bouchard
Mike Hall
Mike Ireland
Sean Ireland
Linda Johnson
Patrick Kelly
Catriona Le May
Ingrid Liepa
Neal Marshall
Michelle Morton
Kevin Scott

Speedskating— Short Track
Frédéric Blackburn
Christine Boudrias
Derrick Campbell
Isabelle Charest
Angela Cutrone
Sylvie Daigle
Marc Gagnon
Stephen Gough
Nathalie Lambert
Denis Mouraux

FINAL MEDAL STANDINGS

(61 events)

NATION	GOLD	SILVER	BRONZE	TOTAL
Norway	10	11	5	26
Germany	9	7	8	24
Russia	11	8	4	23
Italy	7	5	8	20
United States	6	5	2	13
Canada	3	6	4	13
Switzerland	3	4	2	9
Austria	2	3	4	9
South Korea	4	1	1	6
Finland	0	1	5	6
Japan	1	2	2	5
France	0	1	4	5
Netherlands	0	1	3	4
Sweden	2	1	0	3
Kazakhstan	1	2	0	3
China	0	1	2	3
Slovenia	0	0	3	3
Ukraine	1	0	1	2
Belarus	0	2	0	2
Great Britain	0	0	2	2
Uzbekistan	1	0	0	1
Australia	0	0	1	1

Men's 5000 m Speedskating
1. Johann Olav Koss   NOR
2. Kjell Storelid   NOR
3. Rintje Ritsma   NED

Canadians
17. Neal Marshall
22. Neal Marshall

Men's Downhill
1. Tommy Moe   USA
2. Kjetil Andre Aamodt   NOR
3. Edi Podivinsky   CAN

Other Canadians
27. Luke Sauder
31. Ralf Socher

Women's 15 km Freestyle Cross-country
1. Manuela Di Centa   ITA
2. Ljubov Egorova   RUS
3. Nina Gavriluk   RUS

Men's Single Luge
1. George Hacle   GER
2. Mark Prock   AUT
3. A. Zoggeler   ITA

Canadian
20. Clay Ives

Men's 30 km Cross-country Free Technique
1. Thomas Alsgaard   NOR
2. Bjorn Daehlie   NOR
3. Mika Myllylae   FIN

Canadian
51. Dany Bouchard

Men's 500 m Speedskating
1. Aleksandr Golerbev   RUS
2. Sergy Klevchenya   RUS
3. Manabu Horri   JPN

Canadians
11. Sylvain Bouchard
12. Patrick Kelly
17. Sean Ireland
26. Michael Ireland

Men's Combined Downhill
1. Lasse Kjus   NOR
2. Kyle Rasmussen   USA
3. Tommy Moe   USA

Canadians
4. Cary Mullen
5. Edi Podivinsky

Women's 5 km Classical Cross-country Pursuit
1. Ljubov Egorova   RUS
2. Manuela Di Centa   ITA
3. Marja Liisa Kirvesniemi   FIN

Women's Super G
1. Diann Roffe-Steinrotter   USA
2. Svetlana Gladischeva   RUS
3. Isolde Kostner   ITA

Canadians
8. Kerrin Lee-Gartner
12. Kate Pace
25. Michelle Ruthven

Figure Skating — Pairs
1. Ekaterina Gordeeva/
   Sergei Grinkov   RUS
2. Natalya Mishkutenok/
   Artur Dmitriev   RUS
3. Isabelle Brasseur/Lloyd Eisler   CAN

Other Canadians
10. Kristy Sargeant/Kris Wirtz
12. Jamie Salé/Jason Turner

Women's Single Luge
1. Gerda Wiessenteiner   ITA
2. Susi Erdmann   GER
3. Andrea Tagwerker   AUT

Men's 1500 m Speedskating
1. Johann Olav Koss   NOR
2. Rintje Ritsma   NED
3. Falko Zandstra   NED

Canadians
7. Neal Marshall
24. Patrick Kelly
28. Kevin Scott
38. Patrick Bouchard

Women's Moguls
1. Stine Lise Hattestad   NOR
2. Liz McIntyre   USA
3. Elizaveta Kojevnikova   RUS

Canadians
9. Bronwen Thomas
16. Katherina Kubenk

Men's Moguls
1. Jean-Luc Brassard   CAN
2. Serguie Shoupletov   RUS
3. Edgar Grospiron   FRA

Other Canadian
7. John Smart

Men's Classic 10 km Cross-country
1. Bjorn Daehlie   NOR
2. Vladimir Smirnov   KAZ
3. Marco Albarello   ITA

Canadian
49. Dany Bouchard

Men's Super G
1. Markus Wasmeier   GER
2. Tommy Moe   USA
3. Kjetil Andre Aamodt   NOR

Canadians
24. Cary Mullen
26. Brian Stemmle
41. Ralf Socher

Women's 10 km Cross-country Pursuit
1. Lyubov Egorova   RUS
2. Manuela Di Centa   ITA
3. Stephania Belmondo   ITA

Women's 3000 m Speedskating
1. Svetlana Bazhanova   RUS
2. E. Hunyady   AUT
3. Claudia Pechstein   GER

Canadian
14. Ingrid Liepa

Women's Biathlon 15 km
1. Myriam Bédard   CAN
2. Anne Briand   FRA
3. Uschi Disl   GER

Other Canadians
18. Lise Meloche
51. Kristin Berg

Men's 1000 m Speedskating
1. Dan Jansen   USA
2. Igor Zhelerzovsky   BLR
3. Sergey Klevchenya   RUS

Canadians
5. Sylvain Bouchard
6. Patrick Kelly
10. Kevin Scott
16. Sean Ireland

Men's Double Luge
1. Kurt Brugger/WilbertHuber   ITA
2. Hansjord Raffle/Norbert Huber   ITA
3. Stefan Krausse/Jan Behrendt   GER

Canadians
8. Bob Gasper/Clay Ives   CAN

Men's 15 km Cross-country Pursuit
1. Bjorn Daehlie   NOR
2. Vladimir Smirnov   KAZ
3. Sylvio Fauner   ITA

Women's Downhill
1. Katja Seizinger   GER
2. Picabo Street   USA
3. Isolde Kostner   ITA

Canadians
5. Kate Pace
19. Kerrin Lee-Gartner
30. Michelle Ruthven

Women's 500 m Speedskating
1. Bonnie Blair   USA
2. Susan Auch   CAN
3. F. Schenk   GER

Other Canadians
16. Michelle Morton
26. Linda Johnson
33. Catriona Le May

Nordic Combined — 15 km Pursuit
1. Fred Borre Lundberg   NOR
2. Takanori Kono   JPN
3. Bjart Engen Vik   NOR

Men's Figure Skating
1. Alesskei Urmanov   RUS
2. Elvis Stojko   CAN
3. Philippe Candeloro   FRA

Other Canadians
5. Kurt Browning
10. Sébastien Britten

Women's Combined Downhill
1. Katja Seizinger   GER
2. Picabo Street   USA
3. Isolde Kostner   ITA

Canadian
20. Michelle Ruthven

Men's 20 km Biathlon
1. Serguei Tarassov   RUS
2. Frank Luck   GER
3. Sven Fischer   GER

Canadians
43. Steve Cyr
49. Glen Rupertus

Two-Man Bobsleigh
1. Gustav Weder/Donat Acklin   SUI-I
2. Reto Goetschi/Guido Acklin   SUI-II
3. Gunther Heuber/Sefano Ticci   ITA-I

Canadians
7. Pierre Lueders/Dave MacEachern
15. Chris Lori/Glenroy Gilbert

Ski Jumping 120 m
1. Jens Weisflog   GER
2. Espen Bredesen   NOR
3. Andreas Goldberger   AUT

Men's 10 000 m Speedskating
1. Johan Olav Koss   NOR
2. Kjell Storelid   NOR
3. Bart Veldkamp   NED

Women's 4 x 5 km Cross-country Relay
1. Russia
2. Norway
3. Italy

Women's Combined Slalom
1. Pernille Wiberg   SWE
2. Vreni Schneider   SUI
3. Alenka Dovzan   SLO

Women's 1500 m Speedskating
1. E. Hunyady   AUT
2. S. Fedotkina   RUS
3. Gunda Niemann   GER

Canadians
17. Catriona Le May
24. Michelle Morton
28. Ingrid Liepa

Figure Skating — Ice Dance
1. Grichtchuk/Platov   RUS
2. Usova/Zulin   RUS
3. Torvill/Dean   GBR

Canadians
10. Bourne/Kraatz

Men's 4 x 10 km Cross-Country Relay
1. Italy
2. Norway
3. Finland

Team K120 Ski Jump
1. Germany
2. Japan
3. Austria

Women's Short Track 3000 m Speedskating Relay
1. Korea
2. Canada
3. USA

Men's Short Track 1000 m Speedskating
1. Ki-Hoon Kim   KOR
2. Ji-Hoon Chae   KOR
3. Marc Gagnon   CAN

Other Canadians
• Derrick Campbell (NF)
• Frederick Blackburn (DQ)

Women's 7.5 km Biathlon
1. Myriam Bédard   CAN
2. Svetlana Paramygina   BLR
3. Valentyna Tserbe   UKR

Other Canadians
37. Lise Meloche
45. Gill Hamilton

Men's 10 km Biathlon
1. Serguei Tchepikov   RUS
2. Ricco Gross   GER
3. Serguri Tarasson   RUS

Canadians
26. Steve Cyr
62. Glenn Repurtus

Men's Giant Slalom
1. Markus Wasmeier   GER
2. Urs Kaelin   SUI
3. Christian Mayer   AUT

Canadians
16. Thomas Grandi
20. Rob Crossan

Women's 1000 m Speedskating
1. Bonnie Blair   USA
2. Anke Baier   GER
3. Qiabo Ye   CHN

Canadians
8. Susan Auch
19. Catriona Le May
28. Ingrid Liepa (tied)
33. Michelle Morton

Men's Aerials
1. Sonny Schoenbaechler   SUI
2. Philippe LaRoche   CAN
3. Lloyd Langlois   CAN

Other Canadians
4. Andy Capicik
6. Nicholas Fontaine

Women's Aerials
1. Lina Tcherjazova   UZB
2. Marie Lindgren   SWE
3. Hilde Lid   NOR

Canadian
8. Caroline Olivier

Women's Giant Slalom
1. D. Compagnoni   ITA
2. M. Ertl   GER
3. V. Scheider   GER

Canadian
• Melanie Turgeon DNF 2nd run

Women's 30 km Cross-country
1. Manuela Di Centa   ITA
2. Marjut Wold   NOR
3. Maria Kirvesniemi   FIN

Women's 500 m Short Track Speedskating
1. Cathy Turner   USA
2. Yanmei Zhang   CHN
3. Amy Peterson   USA

Men's Combined Slalom

1. Lasse Kjus   NOR
2. Kjetil Andre Aamodt   NOR
3. Harald Christian Nilsen   NOR

Canadians

• Edi Podivinsky   (DNF)
• Cary Mullen   (DNF)

Women's 4 x 7.5 km Biathlon Relay

1. Russia
2. Germany
3. France

Canadians

15. Canada

Individual K90 Ski Jumping

1. Espen Bredesen   NOR
2. Lasse Ottesen   NOR
3. Dieter Thoma   GER

Women's 5000 m Speedskating

1. Claudia Pechstein   GER
2. Gunda Niemann   GER
3. Hiromi Yamamoto   JPN

Canadian

16. Ingrid Liepa

Women's Figure Skating

1. Oksana Baiul   UKR
2. Nancy Kerrigan   USA
3. Lu Chen   CHN

Canadian

9. Josée Chouinard

Women's Slalom

1. Vreni Schneider
2. Elfi Eder
3. Katja Koren

Canadian

• Mélanie Turgeon (DNF first run)

4-Man Bobsleigh

1. GER I   Piloted by Harald Czudaj
2. SUI I   Piloted by Gustav Weder
3. GER II   Piloted by Wolfgang Hoppe

Canadians

9. CAN II Chris Lori, Christian Farstand, Sheridon Baptiste & Glenroy Gilbert
13. CAN I Pierre Lueders, David MacEachern, Jack Pyc & Pascal Caron

Men's 4 x 7.5 km Biathlon Relay

1. Germany
2. Russia
3. France

Women's 1000 m Short Track Speedskating

1. Chun Lee-Kyung   KOR
2. Nathalie Lambert   CAN
3. Kim So-Hee   KOR

Men's 500 m Short Track Speedskating

1. Chae Ji-Hoon   KOR
2. Mirko Vuillerman   ITA
3. Nicholas Gooch   GB

Men's 5000 m Short Track Speedskating Relay

1. Italy
2. USA
3. Australia

Men's Slalom

1. Thomas Stangassinger   AUT
2. Alberto Tomba   ITA
3. Jure Kosir   SLO

50 km Cross-country Classic

1. Vladimir Smirnov   KAZ
2. Mika Myllylae   FIN
3. Stur Siversten   NOR

Hockey

1. Sweden
2. Canada
3. Finland

ACKNOWLEDGEMENTS

This book, like the Olympics, was a team effort. It could not have been completed without the following people whose belief and dedication to this project made it all possible. Gold medals to all—Susan Yates, INFACT Publishing; the CTV Television Network, especially President John Cassaday, Vice President Development and Public Affairs, Counsel-Gary Maavara, Sales Manager, Special Projects-Glen Dickout, Director of Sports-Doug Beeforth, Olympics Co-ordinator-John Shannon, CTV Sports Research-Chris Kapilowski, CTV Archives-Monty Farrell, Manager Corporate Development-Julie Osbourne; Dick Pound-I.O.C.; Dave Rhines; Dave Toms; Don Metz; the Lillehammer Olympic Organizing Committee; the Canadian Olympic Association.

A special thanks to every Canadian athlete who made Lillehammer so compelling, memorable and so very special. Please continue the dream and, by all means, share the spirit!

ROD BLACK

Thanks to Shawn Bowley, Dave Benson, David Rhines of CTV and the indefatigable Dave Toms for additional still photography. Kudos to the whole team-Al Klein, Randy Tomiuk, Dennis Southgate, Mike Dacre, Mike Hayes, Willie Lypko and Richard Willmot.

A special note of appreciation to Glen Sather, President and General Manager of the Edmonton Oilers Hockey Club for his generous support of this project.

D.H. (DON) METZ

PHOTO CREDITS

Lloyd Robertson's
THE NORWEGIAN WAY

CTV's Chief Anchor and Senior News Editor, Lloyd Robertson profiles the country of Norway in a series of short segments, originally shown during the 1994 Olympic Winter Games in Lillehammer, Norway.

Through these segments we see the lifestyles of the Norwegian people who share with us their history and culture. Stories of their hopes, fears and successes help us understand the Norwegian traditions. Lloyd Robertson takes us on a scenic tour of the country, discovering the landscapes, the environment and the people that live in this beautiful country. The Norwegian ideal is to be at peace with the world and at peace with nature, which is clearly captured in Lloyd Robertson's "The Norwegian Way".

ONLY : **$19.99** + GST (Ontario residents add 8% PST)

✂ -

To purchase your own personal copy of Lloyd Robertson's "The Norwegian Way ", fill out this card and send it, along with a cheque or money order to:

**CTV Program & Archive Sales
250 Yonge St., Suite 1800
Toronto, Ontario
M5B 2N8**

☐ I am enclosing a cheque/money order for_____ Norwegian Way videos at $21.39 for each copy. Ontario residents pay $22.99 for each copy.

Name:_____ Phone #_____

Address: _____ Apt. #_____

City:_____ Province:_____ Postal Code:_____

Offer Expires December 31, 1995